AF334741

*Beyond the Ranges*

# BEYOND THE RANGES

## James Stuart Bruce

**VANTAGE PRESS**
New York

To Stevey, Connie, Vicki, and Carolyn,
my constant companions

*Something hidden . . . Go and find it. Go and find it. Go and look beyond the ranges. Something lost beyond the ranges. Something lost beyond the ranges—lost and waiting for you. Go.*

*—Rudyard Kipling*

*Behold, I show you a mystery; we shall not all sleep, but we shall be changed.*

*In a moment, in the twinkling of an eye, at the last trump: for the trumpet shall sound, and the dead shall be raised incorruptible, and we shall be changed.*

—I Corinthians 15:51–52

# **Contents**

# Acknowledgments

I wish to thank the many people who assisted me in writing this book. First and foremost, my wife, whose diligent keeping of diaries helped jog my memory of events that had escaped my mind. Also thanks to Kirk Huffman, director of the Vanuatu Cultural Center at Port Vila, Vanuatu, who was valuable in obtaining permission for me to travel to Pentecost Island to film and record the "land divers." Thanks also to Richard Thiele, a thirty-year resident of Papua New Guinea, for his gracious hospitality on many occasions that made possible my treks into the interior of New Guinea.

Peter Worsely's book, *The Trumpet Shall Sound*, provided me with invaluable information and understanding of "cargo cults," as did many of the native islanders of Malaita (the Solomon Islands) and the people of the village of Warokai on the island of Malaita where my wife and I lived for a period of time. This book is a documentary of filming and exploration over a period of many years in remote areas of the South Pacific that soon will fall prey to western "civilization."

# Introduction

"Something hidden—go and find it—go and look beyond the ranges. Something lost beyond the ranges, lost and waiting for you—go."

During World War II Stuart Bruce was a soldier in New Guinea from 1943–44. Memories of those years haunted and intrigued him so much that he made plans to return and explore the area as soon as time and money would allow.

Starting in 1957 Stu and his wife, Stevey, began exploring the islands of Papua New Guinea, the Solomons, Vanuatu, Fiji, and the Admiralties. They explored and filmed these fascinating islands and their culturally rich people for more than thirty years.

Traveling by boat, jeep and most often on foot, living in native villages and on the trail, they encountered rain, mud, insects, and disease. Stu and Stevey researched, filmed, and studied some of the world's most primitive tribes, cults, and cultures.

This book, *Beyond the Ranges*, tells of excitement and adventure among these people, their strange messianic cults, rituals and the extreme physical problems traveling and living in often unexplored islands and jungles.

Stu, with a Dutch patrol officer and carriers in 1961, penetrated into an unexplored region of Dutch New Guinea (now Irian Jaya) to film rarely seen tribes of the area. It was here, one month later, that anthropologist Mike Rockefeller disappeared under puzzling circumstances.

Throughout the book Stu tells of the mysterious cargo cults found in certain areas of the South Pacific, where in villages natives would destroy their homes, gardens and worldly possessions, build mock airplanes and ships, and sit and await the return of their messiah.

The final chapter tells of the bizarre land divers of Pentecost Island (Vanuatu), which Stu and Stevey filmed, where once a year the men of the island construct eighty-foot wooden towers from where they jump, head first, with only slender vines attached to their ankles to arrest their fall and save them from certain death.

This is the story of the experiences and adventures encountered by Stu and Stevey Bruce in the South Pacific Islands while exploring the strange cults and legends of the peoples of this remote area of the world.


*There is something behind those ranges—go and find it.*

*Beyond the Ranges*

Chapter One

# The War Years

The islands of the South Seas have always been the harborage of many strange and forbidding customs. Headhunting, cannibalism, and witchcraft were common until recently. Perhaps one of the most mystical customs was the cargo cults practiced by the native islanders. These mysterious cults often practiced a degree of self-destruction hard to believe.

World War II opened up the jungle world of the South Pacific to me, and in later years subsequent expeditions to Papua New Guinea, the Solomon Islands, and Vanuatu would reveal to me some of the strange manifestations of these cults that exhibited the frustration and bitterness the native people felt on their exposure to the white man.

In 1944, I was a soldier in the United States Corps of Engineers in the South Pacific on the island of New Guinea. We were preparing for the invasion of Leyte in the Philippine Islands.

By this time the war had bypassed Hollandia* so I whiled away my time sitting entrenched on Red Beach with twenty-five thousand other soldiers awaiting sailing orders.

*The present name of Hollandia is Jayapura. When Indonesia took over control of Dutch New Guinea in 1973, they renamed their western end of the island Irian Jaya.

It wasn't an unpleasant life. We played volleyball, swam, and made occasional forays into the jungle to look for the enemy. Jungle rot and mosquitoes were a big problem, but almost forty years later I remember the experience with a certain amount of nostalgia.

Behind our beach, the vast, brooding, jungle-covered mountains of the Cyclops Range loomed up thousands of feet, their tops almost always covered with heavy clouds. So impenetrable and formidable were these mountains that the war rarely reached this area. Most of the fighting in New Guinea between the Allied troops and the Japanese was along the coast and on the outer islands.

I am only aware of one place in Papua New Guinea, the Kakoda Trail in the Owen Stanley Range, where the Japanese and the Allies fought across the island and in the mountains; there the fight against the elements was as terrible as the war against the enemy.

Between the beach and Lake Sentani a road existed to help supply the Allied airbase, but it penetrated only a few miles inland. Beyond, and to the south, the Cyclops Range climbed to an elevation of over seven thousand feet. Native trails existed in isolated mountain villages, but few Americans ever bothered to follow them.

In my innocence and ignorance, I often conjured up visions of immense poisonous reptiles, dangerous tigers, man-eating lizards, and even prehistoric monsters roaming the swamps and jungles. Later I learned that the most dangerous denizens of the bush were wild pigs and cassowary birds. This is not to minimize the cassawary; a male bird stands three to four feet tall and its powerful claws can disembowel a person with one kick.

The true enemies in New Guinea were not the jungle beasts but the crawling, flying bugs and insects. The dreaded anopheles mosquito, carrier of malaria, probably put as many troops out of action in the South Seas as did battle wounds and death. In later years, I was to suffer severely from malaria. Dengue fever was a scourge, as was typhus. Leeches left open wounds that festered horribly.

The other enemy in New Guinea was the weather. Some New Guinea mountains measured rainfall of two hundred to three hundred inches per year. At Hollandia, on our beach, we once measured fifteen inches in twenty-four hours! If it wasn't too hot, it was too wet. Temperatures along the coast were usually in the high nineties, with the humidity about the same. Despite romantic pictures of South Sea Island paradises, I soon learned that the pictures were quite deceiving. The jungle hid an enemy, but it wasn't only the Japanese.

Few people realize the immensity of New Guinea, the second largest island in the world.* The central highlands of Western New Guinea have been less explored than any other area of the globe. Tribes living in the interior may have yet to see a white man. Cannibalism and headhunting were practiced in many areas and may still be in the isolated interior.

The island is fifteen hundred miles long and about five hundred miles at its widest point. A chain of mountains runs the length of the island from east to west. In that chain there are five peaks over fourteen thousand feet, one topping sixteen thousand feet, with a permanent ice cap. The estimated 2.5 million Melanesian inhabitants often live in such isolated valleys that seven hundred separate and distinct languages have been identified. It can truly be called "the island time forgot."

At Red Beach, surrounded by thousands of other GIs, an amphibious tank unit on one side and a medical hos-

* Greenland is the largest.

pital on the other, it never occurred to me that a native population might be living in the area.

On the troop transport that took us to New Guinea, we were all given a book on Pidgin English and a few rules about how to deal with the natives. However, few of us ever saw natives even after six months in Hollandia.

One day while traveling from Red Beach to Hollandia on an LCM (which was necessary since no bridges existed across Humboldt Bay), a native woman boarded the boat. She was short and naked except for a grass skirt. Her body was smeared with foul-smelling pig grease. Her hair was kinky, her skin jet black, and her breasts hung down like two window shades.

After boarding, she shied away from the soldiers and chose to sit in a corner, eyeing us ruefully. Most of the young girls of the local village had been moved to mountain villages for fear of being raped by the soldiers. A remote fear, it seemed to me, for the native women were most physically unappealing but, as one wag observed, "In six months she'll look like Lana Turner."

The war went on, and I eventually made my way to the Philippines, making the landings on both Leyte and Luzon. On Christmas Day of 1945, Uncle Sam discharged me from service and I joined the civilian ranks once again. I married, established myself in business, and raised three lovely daughters. But a memory continued to haunt me: "What was behind those mountain ranges of New Guinea? What were the people really like?"

Then I was reminded of Rudyard Kipling's famous verse: "Something hidden . . . Go and find it. Go and find it. Go and look beyond the ranges—Something lost behind the ranges—lost and waiting for you. Go." And so I had to go.

## Chapter Two

# Island Hopping

On October 11, 1957, my wife Stevey and I boarded the MV *Malaita*, a thirty-six-hundred-ton Burns Phillip* trading ship, at Sydney harbor, Australia at 3:30 in the afternoon. With us on board were thirty-one other passengers, including traders, missionaries, government workers, and a few children. We were the only tourists. The ship carried an assorted cargo, two jeeps, two fishing boats, an assortment of steel pipes, a boiler tank, drums of muriatic acid, and some reinforcing steel.

For meals, fortunately, we were assigned to the captain's table along with four other women and a man. The captain apparently had scoured the passenger list for the most attractive and youngest women he could find. We were added as something different—Yanks. The skipper, Brett Hilder, was a most remarkable-looking man. He was about forty-five years of age with a big, strapping build, and sported a tremendous, flaming-red handlebar moustache and beard. His reputation was well known and I learned later that in Michener's book *Return to Paradise*, Hilder was one of the five people to whom the book was dedicated.

The dinner was simple but edible and after dinner

*To be referred to as BP in the rest of the book.

we retired to the ship's lounge for coffee, cigars, tales of outback Australia, savage New Guinea, and man-eating sharks and crocs.

I was impressed that several of the passengers had boarded the ship with their golf clubs and tennis rackets to be used in New Guinea and other islands. Civilization wasn't too far away.

Our tiny cabin had two bunks and a wash basin. The toilets were at the end of the passage. In the morning, I found a message scratched on the bedspring of the bunk Stevey occupied above me. It read, "Joe Costello, August 8, 1942. Say a prayer for me, on my way to New Guinea." I learned later that the *Malaita* was torpedoed off Port Moresby on this trip.

Captain Brett, as we sometimes fondly called him, had a roving eye for all the women on board. We further learned that he had a girl friend stashed away in some cabin whom he was delivering to her husband in Brisbane.

The other man at our table, Mr. Way, was a retired government official who had spent most of his life in New Guinea before returning to Sydney. but he couldn't stand "civilization" and decided to return and spend the rest of his retired years back in the "territories," as he put it.

We took on a pilot at noon to guide us into Brisbane harbor, and docked at "Brett's Wharf" at 6:00 P.M., Sunday, October 13. We all gathered on the deck to watch the fun. Mrs. Robertson's husband met her at the wharf, and after a long and very warm farewell between the captain and Mrs. Robertson, with the helpless husband looking on, the unhappy couple finally departed. The rest of us took ourselves to the lounge to gossip about the event.

Monday morning was all too quiet. A dock strike was holding up loading of the ship. We disembarked and went for a stroll through downtown Brisbane. The town had an old, Victorian ambience. Although we were there for a full week, I remember little of the place except for the poor taste the women showed in their quaint clothes and hats.

Stevey and I spent one afternoon with Brett in his cabin, reading his manuscript, which he hoped to have published, while Brett worked on sculpting a piece of wood. I found his style of writing pleasing and he had some remarkable experiences to tell. His account of the eruption of two volcanoes in Rabaul Harbor in 1937 was amazing.

Brett was in the harbor with his ship at the time of the eruption and successfully evacuated six thousand people from the city. Over six hundred people were killed in the explosion. The volcanic ash that settled on the waters of the harbor was so thick he could walk on it!

We milled aimlessly around Brisbane for a week, waiting for the strike to be settled. Finally, on Sunday, October 20, 1957, the *Malaita* set sail north for our "Promised Land." The sea was heavy and the wind stiff, but the weather was warming and a great many flying fish were skimming the Coral Sea.

As the days passed, I learned that the Aussies were the world's greatest beer drinkers. Australian whiskey is harsh, but their beer is excellent, much better than ours. Brett thought nothing of consuming two quarts before a meal, and that was just social drinking. When an Australian settles down to serious drinking, it is as if the world might end on the morrow.

Our ship arrived at Port Moresby at 7:00 A.M., Thursday, October 20. It appeared much prettier and greener than I had expected. At that time in history Moresby (as it is usually called) was the capital city of the Australian Territory of New Guinea. Its jurisdiction included all of

Australian New Guinea, the Admiralty Islands, New Hanover, New Britain, New Ireland, and assorted other islands. It seemed that BP owned much of the town: the dock, the hotel, the refrigeration plant, and other real estate.

Moresby had a population of about four thousand whites and twenty thousand Melanesians, all living within a fifty-mile radius. Twenty-seven miles out of Moresby, on the Kokoda trail, the Japanese army made their deepest land penetration south toward Australia. Here they were stopped by Australian troops (and some Americans) and driven back over the trail in the most primitive fighting conditions encountered in the South Pacific. Frequently the battles took place at elevations of nine thousand to ten thousand feet in dense tropical growth on a trail usually wide enough for only one or two men. The Japanese bombed Moresby often during the war, leaving sunken and beached ships still dotting the coast. The *Malaita* was torpedoed here but with only a small loss of life. It was eventually towed back to Australia and repaired.

The captain managed to obtain a jeep and we drove over to the fishing village of Koka where many natives lived in their lakatois* out in the bay. They would come down from coastal villages on their lakatois to bring fish and food to trade at the local markets. Later we drove over and visited Ward Strip, the airstrip that the Allies used for bombers and fighters during the early days of World War II. We followed the road up along the Hiloki River through country that was impressive in its rugged beauty. Dense jungles surrounded us all the way, many of the trees topping one hundred feet in height.

Our destination was a visit to the Koitaki rubber

* A large, outrigger-style boat with living quarters on the main deck.

plantation. Most of the laborers were young boys and men recruited from the Chimbu highlands in the mountains to the north. They were all heavily tatooed and looked to be in fine physical condition. However, we learned from the Scotsman, who was running the plantation that many were suffering from malaria, an illness not common in the highlands, but prevalent along the coast.

On our return, we visited the Bomona War Memorial Cemetery where five thousand Australians and New Zealanders were buried, killed while fighting in New Guinea and along the Kokoda trail. It was a beautiful cemetery surrounded by colorful shrubs, trees, and carpeted with a manicured green lawn. The crosses were made of a local stone and the entire atmosphere was one of quiet dignity. As I signed the register, I noticed the name of Prince Phillip above mine.

The *Malaita* departed Moresby late at night on October 26, heading for the town of Lae on the northeast coast of New Guinea. We passed through the China Straits on the very eastern tip of the island. This was close to Milne Bay where I spent a brief time in 1944.

After passing through the Straits, the ship headed northwest, and on its way passed close to the Trobriand Islands. The Trobriand islanders have achieved a measure of fame for several reasons: they are consummate wood carvers, among the best in the South Seas, and the subject of a famous book. In 1951, Bronislaw Malinowski, an anthropologist, wrote a book titled *Sex and Regression in Savage Society,* which dealt almost entirely with the unusual sexual practices of the Trobriand Islanders. Passing the islands allowed Brett time to discourse on this book and its subject matter with the ladies at the table. He enjoyed the shock effect.

Sunday morning, October 27, finally brought us into Lae harbor, a small city of about two thousand people on the northeast coast of New Guinea. Here was the real New Guinea: dense, lush jungles, and steaming heat. One could smell the rancid odor of decaying vegetation drifting out to sea. Lae is the principal terminus for planes flying into the highlands. Most of the gold from Bulolo placer mines passed through here.* Bulolo, a town in the Highlands, also developed a plywood industry based on the harvesting of the Klinkii pine tree and the wood was transported to Lae for shipment abroad. Lae had been the scene of heavy fighting during the war and the coastline was dotted with wrecked landing barges, ships, and rusting tanks.

One evening a crocodile came swimming out beside the ship. He was big and awesome-looking, apparently looking for food. When he smelled the chow being cooked on board the *Malaita*, he fled in horror and disgust, probably deciding that the small boys fishing on the local river were a better entrée.

All the next day we sailed off the Maclay coast of New Guinea with a magnificent view of the Finisterre Range to the south. Some of the Finisterre peaks reach a height of thirteen thousand feet. The ship was making thirteen knots with favorable tides. We reached the harbor of Madang at noon.

Madang turned out to be one of the prettiest New Guinea harbors that I have seen. I still cherish a watercolor painting that Brett Hilder had made and presented to us of the bay. Its population was about eight hundred Europeans and an unknown number of natives. The town was clustered around the shores of a many-armed coral headland, and the town, with its shady drives and waving

* These gold mines have long been mined out. It was the prospect of working the gold fields that brought Errol Flynn to New Guinea in 1930.

palm trees, was mixed up with the harbor and the lagoon. After taking the launch to shore, we spent some time visiting the Lutheran Mission and the Chinese shops. After lunch, at the local pub, we met Brett at BP's and strolled on the beautiful golf course. Adjoining the golf course was a bowling green, and nearby were two tennis courts made of crushed coral.

That evening Brett invited Stevey and me to join him on a visit to Mr. and Mrs. Pims' home. Brett seemed to have a special attachment to us. The other passengers were not invited to most of these soirees. The Pims had a lovely home (by New Guinea standards) surrounded by a beautiful garden. Three native boys worked for them as cook, houseboy, and gardener. They lived by a golf course and had their own private beach. In addition, the house had a refrigerator, electric range, running water, and a bath and shower. Mr. Pims had lived in New Guinea for thirty-two years, most of the time as an employee of BP's. He paid no taxes, and received a vacation of three months for every two and a half years of service. He was also a director of the Bulolo Gold Mining Company, and for as long as he had been associated with the company he had been receiving a yearly dividend of 120 percent!

After numerous beers and a good dinner, we retired to the screened-in front porch to listen to the many stories that the Pims had to tell of their experiences through the years living in primitive New Guinea. I later learned that many of the stories white settlers told were "hand-me-downs" with questionable authenticity.

One of the true stories that the Pims told was of the natives' seeming indifference to pain and injury to themselves and to others. Natives would often laugh and joke when they saw another person badly injured and make no effort to help. Often a badly injured person would not be allowed to return to the village for fear he would just become another burden on their time and food supply.

We saw an example of this when we drove out to visit the native hospital the next day. It was a simple place with a dirt floor and wooden planks for beds. One native male patient had been hit on the head with an ax during a fight and cut from ear to ear, but he appeared quietly resigned and headed for recovery. I asked the doctor if there wasn't a likelihood of brain damage and he replied, "These natives don't have any brains anyway, so it won't make any difference." This was not an unusual attitude among many of the white settlers, who regarded most of the native people as "simple savages," not much cut above an animal.

*Chapter Three*

# The Admiralty Islands

The *Malaita* departed mainland New Guinea and headed
north on October 31. Our destination was the town of
Lombrom on Manus. Manus Island is in the middle of the
Bismarck Sea, so named by the early German settlers
and explorers.* It belongs to a group of islands called the
Admiralties, well known to American troops during World
War II and where the First Cavalry Division saw some
of its first action.

During the war, American Seabees constructed huge
naval and military bases on Manus with quarters for
about fifty thousand soldiers, complete with floating dry
docks, cranes, workshops, repair facilities, swimming
pools, theaters, et cetera. They also built roads and
brought in jeeps, heavy trucks and construction equipment.

The story is told that after the war ended, the American government offered the whole "kit and caboodle" to
the Australian government for a bargain price. When the
Aussies refused, the Yanks offered it to them again, this
time for a token price. The Aussies again refused, believ-
ing they would get it for nothing. Uncle Sam got peeved
and sold the whole lot to the Chinese Nationalist government who shipped it off to Taiwan.

* The Germans once ruled this area before World War I.

One incident happened to me on Manus that shall be forever etched in my memory. The base commander, whom we met through Brett, took us to a lovely beach for a swim, the day being incredibly hot and humid. Here I enjoyed a swim, peering through goggles at the many-colored reef fish. On my way in, however, I made the mistake of stepping on a sea urchin and came out with my foot loaded with sharp spines. The commander assisted me into his jeep and rushed me over to the base hospital. At this point, the spines had broken off, but the points were still in my foot causing me considerable pain. The commander explained to me that the removal of the spines was going to be quite painful and proffered me a full glass of whiskey to try and help ease the painful extraction the medic was about to perform. I downed this and in a few moments was bleary-eyed. At this point, the commander laughed and said, "Actually, those spines will have dissolved in your foot by tomorrow and we don't have to do anything about removing them!" The following day I nursed a slightly swollen foot and a powerful headache.

Our visit to Lombrom was brief and the next day the *Malaita* headed out to sea once again with Lorengau as her destination, a small port on the same island of Manus. The sky was cloudless and the blazing sun beat unremittingly on us.

At about two o'clock in the morning, while under way, Stevey and I were awakened by an extremely violent shaking of the ship. This was repeated and we rushed up on deck with other passengers. My first thought was that the ship had run onto a reef, one of the terrors of sailors in this region. However, the ship kept on its way and the rest of the night passed without incident. Next morning at breakfast, Brett informed us that we had experienced a "guira," an underwater volcanic explosion, not uncommon in this area.

It was now the first of November. At this latitude* it didn't make much difference as it was always hot and humid. Lorengau was the smallest community we had visited thus far. It had no docking facilities. All loading and unloading had to be done by lighters, which were towed to and from the ship by motor boats.

When the lighters reached the shore, natives had to wade out, hoist the loads to their backs, and stumble ashore through a rough surf to the warehouse. Our ship was taking on a load of copra. This load was adding a foul stench to the *Malaita*, which did not quite drown out the more powerful smell of the curry and rice that the cook was preparing for our dinner.

We spent most of the morning shopping at the local marketplace. Besides the usual foodstuffs of bananas, fish, octopus, there was a profusion of seashells. Some of the most beautiful shells in the world can be found in the water around Manus. The natives put a high value on them for they are still used for decorative purposes and as a sign of wealth.

The natives sat on their haunches with their produce stacked in front of them, chasing the flies away and chewing on betelnut. Mixed with lime, the betelnut is a popular chew for both men and women. It is slightly narcotic, but its worst effect is the permanent red stain it leaves on the teeth and gums.

It was a colorful market. Natives were seated all over the grounds. Many were selling live possums caged in baskets, smoked octopus, crabs wrapped in nets, fruit,

*About three degrees north of the equator.

baby sharks, turtle eggs, and sago, the ever-faithful diet. The many baldheaded and barebreasted women, their mouths stained a brilliant red from betelnut, and tattooed from head to foot, sat and kibbitzed the morning away.

Now completely ensconced in Brett's good favor, we joined him for a visit to the District Commissioner, Ted Hicks. Ted's home was located on a hillside near the waterfront, with a beautiful garden full of fragrant cocoa trees and hibiscus bushes. Ted invited us in for a drink, a habit that preceded every meal except breakfast. Our first duty was to sign the government book. Our names joined those of General MacArthur, Eleanor Roosevelt, General Sims, and others.

The bathtub at Government House (usually called the Residency) was built especially for Carol Landis when she visited during the war to entertain the troops. Ted invited us to stay for a party that evening. Brett, who had just put away his fourth quart of beer, was sorely tempted to hold the ship over. However, BP's image loomed too strongly in the background to accept. It was fortunate that we were not docked at the wharf for I seriously doubt whether Brett could have come away without half the wharf dangling on the ship's superstructure.

It was now November 3, and the ship was sailing a slightly unsteady course toward Kavieng, New Ireland. The ship had to pass through the straits between New Hanover and New Ireland—a very tricky passage strewn with the remains of ships wrecked on reefs. New Ireland was discovered by William Dapier in 1699, but much of the island's coastline was not surveyed until Brett Hilder did so in 1939.

Close to Kavieng Harbor was the island of Nusalik where, according to local historians, the Japanese had executed twenty-eight Australian "coastwatchers" by beheading them. In the waters directly in front of the island were two partially submerged Japanese transport ships. Their rusted bridges and twisted masts reminded us of the fury of the Allied air raid that must have caught them there as they tried to escape the harbor back in 1944.

A famous landmark at Kavieng is the tomb of Balaminski, the German district officer of the territory when this part of New Guinea was under German control. According to legend, Balaminski had such a dynamic personality that he alone was responsible for taming the fierce natives, building roads, and establishing plantations. He typified, at its best or worst, the early German colonizers—ambitious, ruthless, and determined. Rather surprisingly, the natives of the territory held the Germans in high esteem. The Germans (for those natives who could still remember) were considered to be firm and just masters.

To reach Rabaul, New Britain, the ship had to sail almost due South. We arrived there at 6:00 A.M., November 5. Rabaul is on the northern end of the Island of New Britain and had a population of three thousand whites and two thousand Chinese. I find it strange and interesting that so many of my notes include no mention of indigenous people. Obviously, Australian records paid little attention to this fact. As it turned out, I discovered, there is a large population of Chinese merchants throughout the islands. Their ancestors came to work for the old German colonizers, and most of them are now well-established as shop owners, traders, and successful businessmen.

Rabaul harbor is situated in a large bay ringed by seven volcanoes, one still active. In 1937, one of these volcanoes, called "Vulcan," exploded violently and buried the city and parts of the bay with ash. Over six hundred people were killed in the eruption. Brett's ship was anchored out in the bay at the time it happened and he assisted in evacuating over six thousand people. Rabaul is still frequently shaken by earthquakes and the town is not considered to be safe from future volcanic eruptions. Cinder ash from thousands of years has made the land around Rabaul the richest in New Guinea. At the time we were there in 1957, Rabaul ws successfully exporting copra and cocoa, and possessed one of the best established European societies. There was a large Chinatown where one could cheaply buy all sorts of Asian goods never seen in Australia.

During the war, the Japanese captured Rabaul from the Australians and established a huge naval base. Although the Allies never tried to recapture Rabaul, because it was considered impregnable, they bombed it almost daily for three years. As a result, the Japanese went underground. All of their repair shops, gun positions, living quarters and storage were placed in huge caves and tunnels in the sides of hills, all much in evidence even today. Although the bombing didn't inflict great loss of life, it completely flattened the town and hundreds of ships were sunk in the harbor. Thousands of Japanese troops were stationed at Rabaul during the war. When Japan surrendered in 1945 and the Australians moved in, they found most of the Japanese existing under starvation conditions.

That evening we were invited to the popular New Guinea Club for dinner. Here was the perfect example of civilization that the white man had brought to the tropics. A large party was in progress and the ladies and gentlemen were all impeccably attired in formal evening dress, despite the ninety-degree heat. Barefoot native boys dressed in comfortable *lap-laps* (a wraparound skirt) were drifting among the guests, serving champagne and gin fizzes. Unfortunately, since I did not have a coat and tie I was asked to sit on the veranda with my wife to eat our dinner. After the dinner and dancing, the men retired to their private lounge to be served cigars and brandy. The women went to the parlor to gossip.

At this point, we decided to leave the ship and fly up to the New Guinea Highlands, an area reputed to be of great beauty. We moved to the Hotel Cosmopolitan, the original "fleabag" of the world. We sat on the veranda and watched the *Malaita* depart Rabaul harbor. The sea was quiet and the stars sparkled like diamonds on black velvet. Since that time we have corresponded with Brett and visited him in Australia.*

* Brett is now dead after being distinguished as an artist, author, sculptor, and skipper.

## *Chapter Four*

# New Guinea Highlands

Rabaul was hot and humid with little to encourage us to stay except for the murky hotel swimming pool. We used it disastrously, as time would tell. Boarding the next flight available to Goroka, we flew west, crossing the Bismarck Sea, and on to mainland New Guinea near the vicinity of Lae.

Our DC-3 flew over the Finisterre Range of mountains. Some of its peaks reach over ten thousand feet. We were airborne with three other passengers, a load of clay pipes, chicken wire, and tomato sauce, all in the same cabin. Going to Goroka to the New Guinea Highlands in 1957 meant taking any flight available, for no roads existed to the interior.

Now one can fly to Goroka in comfortable, pressurized planes or take a leisurely drive up the Markham Valley road. There are numerous small hotels along the way with plenty of beer and adequate cuisine. Natives will leave their coffee plantations, drive over to the hotel in their own trucks, and, for a few bucks, take off their T-shirts and shorts, don their feathers and war paint, and give a whopping good Sing-Sing, the traditional native dance. Then they'll go home, light up a cigarette, and have a good laugh about the tourists they saw that day.

However, Goroka today is somewhat different than when we were first there in 1957 and greatly changed from what it must have been like when first discovered by European gold prospectors when they first explored it in 1934.

As we approached Goroka's landing strip we could see the vast Whagi Valley spread out before us, its floor dotted with numerous farms and plantations and cut by myriad rivers. Small villages with thatched native huts were scattered across the valley, smoke eddying out of their rooftops.

After establishing ourselves at the local hotel (often called a pub) we made our usual reconnaissance of the town. Since it was a Saturday afternoon, the traditional market day for the village, great streams of natives were flocking into Goroka to shop or sell their goods at the marketplace. It was not unlike marketplaces throughout the world in predominantly agricultural societies, except for the people. They were unique.

Most of the Kanakas* were dressed in all their splendor, their bodies covered with pig's grease and mud, their headdresses resplendent with birds of paradise feathers, leaves, flowers, and other plumage. On their chests they wore necklaces of cowrie shells, beads, or possum tails. Through their noses were inserted pig's tusks or cassowary quills. Although the nights in the Highlands can get quite cold, most of the men wore only a flimsy sporan or bark string over their scrotum.

The women wore grass skirts and an assortment of shells and beads as necklaces. The older women all had sagging bare breasts and an overworked appearance. While the young girls were physically attractive, most had spoiled their looks with ugly stains of betelnut on their teeth.

Most of these brown-skinned Melanesians were quite

* A common name for natives, but considered derogatory now.

short, the average man not much over five feet in height. Body tattooing was common as were "welt" designs on the body. This was achieved by cutting the skin and stuffing clay in the wound. When the wound healed over, it left a strangely attractive, lumpy design.

At the pub we met three Australians who were about to embark on a flight up to the Whagi Valley. They agreed to let us join them and share the cost of the charter. One was a patrol officer, the others were plantation owners. We took off from Goroka airstrip, flew through a nine-thousand foot pass across the Bismarck mountains and east toward the Dutch New Guinea (Irian Jaya) border.

The floor of this immense valley that we passed over was not even known to exist by Europeans until 1934. It was crisscrossed with mountain rivers rushing down to the ocean, and its rolling hills were covered with high kunai grass. The valley was lush green, but almost treeless. On both sides great mountains rose—Mount Wilhelm almost fifteen thousand feet high and Mount Michael only slightly lower. Below, we saw many communal farms worked by the natives. There was one road running between Goroka and Mount Hagen and we could see it winding along the river floor. It was used mainly by truckers carrying foodstuffs and other goods to various outposts. This road was built and maintained by native labor under Australian supervision. The road served the native population for a purpose because it allowed them to bring their market goods into Goroka and carry back trade store goods. A road is easier to walk than a mountain trail and there was always the chance of a lift on a passing truck. The natives did not disdain convenience. This remarkable road had been constructed by gangs of men, women, and children using picks and shovels, and on occasion, sharpened sticks. There were a few bridges and most streams and rivers had to be either forded or the vehicles "rafted" across. When the rains were heavy, which was often, outposts were isolated for days.

Without doubt, the introduction of the road rapidly changed the lives of the natives. Australian patrol officers entered the village political-social life (for good or bad), assisting in settling intertribal and intervillage disputes. (That's the way it was in the old colonial days.) The roads permitted the visit of medical officers and the chance to trade pigs, garden produce, and prospective brides with more distant villages. Eventually, it opened the area to coffee and tea plantations.

On the way to Mount Hagen, we stopped at a tiny dirt airstrip to let off one of our passengers. All I could see was a small native village and one building that had been constructed for storage purposes. Our disembarking passenger went to the warehouse, unlocked it, pulled out his motorbike, and drove off. Inasmuch as it was a fairly warm day and we were in no particular hurry, we got our sandwiches out of the plane and sat under the wing to enjoy lunch.

In no time, a small crowd of curious, naked little boys gathered. Shortly, they were joined by a group of potbellied, almost naked women, and finally a few of the village elders came over to have a look. The men were extremely fierce looking, carrying axes, their heads bedecked with plumage, faces stained with charcoal and pigs' tusks thrust through their noses. They were most curious about the large bandage that Stevey was wearing over her eye because of an infection incurred at the pool in Rabaul. They studied and discussed her for a long time.

Finally, tired of being stared at and measured for our protein content, we climbed aboard the plane and took off for Mount Hagen. Hagen, for all purposes, was the end of the valley and the end of the road. Anyone wishing to proceed westward from there toward the Dutch New Guinea border would have to do so on foot and with Australian patrols. From here on, the country was considered "uncontrolled" and native warriors might give any visitors a nasty reception.

While at the pub in Goroka, I made the acquaintance of Patrol Officer Holmes, who, after a few beers, agreed to take us out on a Land Rover trip through his "district." We started out in the early morning along the "highland road," as it is generously called, which goes out in a southeasterly direction from Goroka to Bena Bena. Patrol Officer Holmes told us that he had about 105,000 people living in his district and that his duties were to try and settle village disputes that the village elders felt they couldn't cope with, make arrests when necessary, hold trials, and to see that the road was maintained.

Stevey and I sat in the front seat of the Land Rover with Holmes. In back were six native policemen who looked impressive in their black *lap-lap* uniforms and black berets trimmed in red. The only weapons in evidence were bayonets hanging from scabbards around their waists. They were barefoot as were all of the natives in this area.

As we traveled, we would encounter groups of locals working on the road. Each group represented one particular village's "one day a week" contribution to road maintenance. Whenever we arrived at a village, the "head man" would present himself to Holmes and offer a snappy military salute—quite amusing to see when the man had a pig's tusk thrust through his nose and no clothes on. Soon most of the villagers collected around the car. Then began a lengthy parley, conducted in pidgin, between Holmes and the head man. This had to be done through an interpreter as none of the villagers spoke pidgin.

Pidgin (sometimes erroneously called Pidgin English) is the *lingua franca* of most of the South Seas and New Guinea. It is generally spoken between Europeans and natives and often between natives, except in the most remote villages where local dialects prevail. Pidgin is easy to learn, and on an island where you have seven hundred languages, there has to be some common voice.

The problems that Holmes had to cope with were many and varied. In one instance, a villager complained to Holmes that he had planted coffee trees with the understanding that the rest of the village would share in the labor and the profits. However, it seemed that only his family was contributing any time to tending the trees. Holmes pidgin answer was quite simple, "Em fella no work, em no gat money."

In another instance, a woman complained that her husband had deserted her. She had found another man who was willing to pay her father four pigs for her and she was happy with this arrangement. The village elders had decided that this was okay, but wanted the patrol officer's approval. He gave it.

The ownership of pigs in New Guinea, even today, shows a man's wealth and enhances his prestige in his village or tribe. Only the most sophisticated coastal dwellers could afford to ignore this important socio-economic custom. A Highland man buys his wife with pigs, honors his friends with pig feasts, and pays his debts with pigs. For thousands of years, the people of New Guinea have suffered from a protein shortage. The island simply did not have enough edible game animals, except pigs. However, pigs were also scarce so they were hoarded, protected, loved and treated as one of the family and allowed free run of the house. It was not uncommon to see a woman nursing her baby on one breast, with a baby pig on the other. The pig is considered to be as valuable in the family

as any child. Woe betide the woman who allowed a pig
to become sick and die. This would surely bring a beating
from her husband.

The greatest honor that a man could bestow upon
himself, his family or his village was to throw a huge pig
feast where all the important people from other villages
were invited. The more pigs killed and eaten the greater
his prestige. These feasts were infrequent and between
feasts little meat was eaten. Cattle and canned meats
have now been introduced throughout the island, perhaps
bringing an end to this ancient custom.

On another day, Holmes took us to a prison that he
helped maintain. There, ten prisoners were locked up.
They were all murderers, serving from three- to seven-year
sentences. The prison turned out to be nothing more than
a group of small thatched huts with no locks or bars.

The prisoners did their own cooking and maintained
a garden for their food. They were not closely guarded;
only one policeman seemed to be in evidence. If a prisoner
were to successfully escape, the police would easily find
him for it would be almost certain that he would return
to his village. It would be unthinkable for a native to find
refuge in a village other than his own. So strongly ingrained was the fear between tribes that it was
difficult to expect men from different villages to consider
working alongside one another.

Murder was not looked upon as too serious a crime,
as long as it was not committed against a European. The
Australian authorities recognized the fact that most native murders were done in fits of rage, usually to avenge
some real or imagined tribal feud. Historically, these
people have lived in such isolation from each other, because of high mountains and deep valleys separating
them, that anyone outside of their own particular village

was considered a dangerous threat. The problem that Australian authorities were faced with at that time was trying to convince the people that they must quit their frequent wars and accept some sort of law and order.

Stevey's eye infection had worsened and she had gone to the hospital. In the meantime, I made arrangements with Johnny, another patrol officer, to go on a road patrol. Our destination was Rintepe, southwest of Goroka. Again, we traveled in a Land Rover with six native policemen. This particular road was quite narrow, twisting, and turning. As the day before, our approach to the village was greeted by large crowds of natives who gathered around the truck for parley. The patrol officer and the chief did most of the talking, while the villagers watched with rapt attention. The weather had turned cold and rainy, and the almost naked men stood with their arms wrapped around their shoulders, shivering from the cold.

Johnny did his best, but he was an inexperienced cadet patrol officer and the village elders were not impressed by him, largely ignoring his advice. We drove out of the hamlet at a high rate of speed. Suddenly, we came upon a mother with her three children and a pig standing in the middle of the road. The frightened mother, completely ignoring her three children, rushed to the pig and hauled it out of harm's way.

During the afternoon, Johnny and I stopped at another native village and were invited by the chief to join him in his hut for a cup of tea. The hut was quite low, with an umbrella-shaped roof, a dirt floor and a small fire burning in the center of the floor. It was so smoky, I could hardly breathe.

We sat cross-legged on the floor in the company of four village elders sipping strong black tea. The chief's four daughters sat, barely visible in the smoky background, watching us with rapt attention.

One of the daughters, a flat-bellied, full-breasted, and gaily decorated young lady of about thirteen was eyeballing me quite boldly. I was on the verge of striking up a friendship until the odor of pig's grease assailed my nose. The romance drifted out the open door, as I did. As we left, I exchanged glances with little "pickaninny pig's grease," but at that point she seemed more interested in trying to thrust a cassowary quill through her nose.

*Chapter Five*

# Dutch New Guinea

After our return from New Guinea in 1957 a number of years went by, but I was still intent on returning to New Guinea. Suddenly the opportunity presented itself.

I had the good fortune to meet Dr. Victor de Bruyn while I was attending a World Affairs Council meeting in Los Angeles in 1959. Dr. de Bruyn had gained considerable fame during World War II by living among the indigenous people of Dutch New Guinea and sending out radio messages to the Australians and the Americans of Japanese troop movements. At the time I met Victor, he was still working for the Dutch government and still actively involved in Dutch New Guinea affairs. Introducing myself to Dr. de Bruyn, I explained that I had been stationed in Hollandia during the war and would like to return for a visit, asking his assistance.

At that time, Dutch New Guinea was off-limits to tourists and a special permit was needed to enter. Sukarno and his Indonesian government were waging a desultory war against the Dutch to gain control over the territory, which eventually succeeded. It was not by strength of arms, however, for the Indonesians were being easily outfought by the Dutch troops. The administration of the territory was costing the Dutch government in the Netherlands so much money that they saw no reason to throw good money after bad and fight a war to boot.

Dr. de Bruyn did arrange our permits and on January 29, 1960, we found ourselves headed back to the South Pacific with Hollandia as our goal. Our trip took us by way of Sydney, Port Moresby, and Lae. We stopped over for a few days in Lae to visit our friends from a previous trip, Sue and Norm Osborn.

They entertained us royally at their plantation and we enjoyed quantities of Chinese food and greater quantities of beer. On February 3, we departed Lae in a DC-3, flying in a northwesterly direction, passing over the coast towns of Madang, Wewak, and Aitape, finally reaching Hollandia in the early afternoon. The airstrip was located at Lake Sentani, some miles out of Hollandia. We found a bus that took us into town and to our hotel, a sorry-looking dump by any standards.

Driving through town, I was reminded of my stay there sixteen years before. There didn't seem to be much improvement, and the same old quonset huts were still in use, but just looking shabbier. The natives in the town were all dressed in T-shirts and shorts, still without shoes and appeared sullen and disconsolate. The next morning we had our first exposure to a Dutch breakfast: chocolate chips on white bread and strong black coffee. The few guests in the hotel were mostly businessmen, eager to leave as soon as possible. The weather was hot and humid, blessed occasionally by a coolish breeze off Humboldt Bay. The hotel help moved around in a state of torpidity, as I did.

I was anxious to visit Red Beach, my home for six months during the war. Since no boats were going that way, I filmed it from afar through a telephoto lense. It appeared lonely and deserted. My memories drifted back to the days when I and twenty-five thousand men lived there for at least half a year, isolated from the rest of the world. A few days later, I was on the beach and wondered, *How the hell did twenty-five thousand men ever live here?*

Dr. Gallis, a government official, offered us a drive around town, which we accepted with alacrity since we were getting bored with inactivity. By good fortune, Dr. de Bruyn was in town, so we visited with him and received a good briefing on conditions in Dutch New Guinea and the state of the ongoing war with Indonesia. I asked him about the possibilities of the Indonesians mounting an invasion from the mainland. He laughed and said, "Their whole army is going to have to learn how to swim, because their navy doesn't have any boats."

After lunch with Dr. Gallis, we were required to go to the government hospital for X-rays. Since there were then no known cases of TB in the Highlands, the health authorities weren't about to allow any infected persons in. The hospital itself was brand new and fairly well-equipped. It had 350 beds, a staff of Dutch and native nurses, and eight full-time doctors.

For a while, I was afraid that this visit to Hollandia might turn out to be a flop and that we might be isolated here with no place to go and nothing to do. So many of the available aircraft had been diverted to ferrying troops and supplies to the western tip of New Guinea to counter the Indonesian threat that not many flights were going into the Highlands. However, our luck held. A Canadian aircraft company was demonstrating a new airplane, the Caribou, and had sent it around the world on a sales exposure tour. It had landed at Lake Sentani the day after we arrived to demonstrate its versatility at high altitudes and on short strips. We were invited to go along by the district commissioner as guests of the government and also offered a short stay at the government patrol post in the Baliem Valley. The commissioner warned us that because of weather conditions, always unpredictable, we might be forced to stay longer than we cared. My only hope was that it might be so.

Dr. Gallis introduced us to a young government official who was to act as our guide and companion for the few days we had in Hollandia. His name was Jaap Lind. He was to have a profound effect on our lives for the next five years—not all of it pleasant.

In the morning, Jaap took us out in a government patrol boat to visit some of the villages that had been built out over the water among the many surrounding islands in Humboldt Bay. Jaap stopped at one seaborn village where we paid a visit. In one house, we found a woman in a darkened room lying on the floor, visibly very ill. Jaap questioned the family and learned she was dying of TB. When questioned as to why the woman had not been sent to the hospital, the family members giggled and looked embarrassed but offered no answer. We were to learn later that those dying prefer to do so at home. A doctor would order them to the hospital. There seemed to be no idea in the family of the possibility of their catching her disease.

Jaap was full of information, and over a cup of hot tea that afternoon, he told us some interesting stories about the territory. We learned that to the south and beyond the fifteen-thousand foot Carstenz Range, the island drops away to the most brutal swamps and jungles. The people of this area were, by reputation, the fiercest of all New Guinea natives, and headhunting was still quite common as was cannibalism. The people of this area, known as the Asmat, spent much of their life hunting, fishing, raiding and warring, traveling about in their forty-foot canoes. Each canoe prow was decorated with a magnificent carving representing a mythological creature. It was in search of these carvings that Mike Rockefeller met his untimely death.

In the evening, the district commissioner again invited us to tea and schnapps. He explained to us that flying into the Baliem Valley could be difficult and dangerous, especially in a new aircraft. The mountains were high, the valley itself stood at six thousand feet, and clouds and rain in the afternoons created a real flying hazard. Since there were no roads, there was no other choice. The DC had been a prisoner in Burma during the war and worked on the infamous "Bridge on the River Kwai." He attributed his survival to the fact that he had served as a patrol officer in New Guinea and the life there had toughened him far beyond that of the other soldiers. A few other bits of information that were thrown out during the course of the afternoon only added spice to the stories describing the peoples of New Guinea.

Perhaps the best told story was of the bush pilot who was flying his plane from Hollandia to Wewak. The plane developed engine trouble as it was approaching the landing strip. The pilot told his native passenger (who was on his first flight) to be prepared to jump as soon as he hit the strip, since he was afraid that a fire might ensue. On the final approach, the plane clipped the tops of some palm trees with its lowered wheels—this was enough for the native. He opened the door and jumped, crashing down through the tree branches, landing only slightly bruised and cut. The plane hit the trees and was suspended in the branches with the pilot hanging out, held only by his seat strap. The rescuing crew from Wewak observed the native walking past the suspended pilot without ever turning his head. He apparently thought this was standard operating procedure!

Every so often, the Dutch authorities would fly village chiefs from remote mountain villages down the coast, attempting to impress them with the white man's wealth and power. Most of the chiefs seemed not too awed by the airplanes. They considered them birds the whites had tamed. What did impress them, however, was the ocean, which they considered to be the end of the world. When they tasted the salty ocean water, they had to be forcibly stopped from drinking too much. Salt was a rare commodity in the highlands with a tremendous value attached to it. The native chiefs were convinced of the wealth and power of the Dutch, not for their airplanes, automobiles, fine homes and big ships, but for their oceans of valuable salt.

The District Resident came for us at 6:00 A.M. and drove us out to the Sentani airstrip. An early start would be necessary before the clouds, wind, and rain began to build up around the mountain ridges. The Caribou was a large, twin-engined aircraft with a top speed of 175 miles per hour, a capacity of about fifty passengers, and a reputation for being able to land and take off at high altitudes on short strips. These were the exact conditions at Post Baliem where the altitude was six thousand feet and the grass strip dangerously short. This was to be a unique flight since the previous planes flying into the Highlands were nothing larger than Cessna 180s.

The flight took about one and a half hours and the scenery below was spectacular. The jungle looked impassable by foot, but there may have been some native trails. There were many rivers flowing through deep valleys, and occasionally one could see tiny villages perched on top of precipitous limestone ridges. As we approached the Baliem Valley far to the south, we caught glimpses of the mighty Carstenz mountains with their glacier-capped peaks.

The plane landed without incident and was immediately surrounded by dozens of excited natives who had assembled to catch a glimpse of the strange, new "big white bird." Although the natives in this area were fairly used to seeing the mission and government aircraft landing, all these planes were tiny compared to this monster.

As I left the aircraft along with the others, we were immediately engulfed by an excited throng of natives who touched and pulled our clothes and hair. Being bald, I was an even greater oddity. The sight of us brought forth guttural "ohs" and "ahs" from the assembled throng.

The men surrounding us were completely nude except for their *holims* (penis sheaths), an elongated gourd that often rose vertically to the shoulders of the wearer and was held erect by a fiber thread round the chest. The gourds were probably worn as a phallic symbol, as well as for protection. Their bodies were smeared with pigs' grease for warmth and pigs' tusks or shells were thrust through the septum of the nose. The women wore fiber skirts and had large nets attached to a headband flung over the back. These were used to carry babies and garden vegetables.

Stevey, the only woman in our group, created an uproar as she disembarked from the plane. The men clicked at their gourds furiously while the women let out a series of wailing sounds, half in delight, half in awe.

The plane dallied for only a short time, because of worsening weather conditions, so all of the passengers reembarked and the plane took off for Hollandia. We, by good fortune, were allowed to stay at Post Baliem.

Our home for the next week was the patrol house and our hosts were Jan and Margriet Broekhuyse, a young Dutch couple. Jan was the Dutch patrol officer in command. Jan was to create quite a stir by his actions in the

Baliem, which cost him his job, as I will explain later. The settlement of Post Baliem (now called Wanema) was situated on a riverbank and consisted of almost half a dozen corrugated tin buildings and was staffed by four Europeans and thirty native police.

I found out later, much to my dismay, that the Broekhuyses did not welcome our visit. Heavy rains had flooded the Baliem Valley for weeks, making it difficult to fly in food supplies. Native gardens had been badly flooded, ruining their yam and potato gardens. A real food crisis existed. We were not aware of this at the time but sensed a note of hostility from our hosts. However, we were guests of the Dutch government and "that was that."

The Baliem Valley, sometimes known as the Grand Valley, is about ten miles wide and fifty miles long with a population of about seventy-five thousand known as the Dani people. Within the valley most of the natives engaged in year-round disputes and war with one another, often with their closest neighbors. They love to fight and war was treated as a sport with rules of combat to be strictly observed. The battles were fought on prearranged battle grounds. Much shouting and hurling of insults preceded the affair. When the warriors finally joined in battle, they did so in short rushes at each other, hurling spears and firing arrows. Such was the agility of these men that most spears and arrows were dodged; however, death and injuries did occur. For the Dani, a balance of casualties on both sides was usually satisfactory, but there was always the "next time" when a death or injury, a stolen pig, a raped woman, or a personal insult had to be avenged. All of this is now banned by the Indonesian government.

Jan Broikhuyse's problem started when, as a district

officer at Post Baliem in 1962, he allowed a Peabody Museum team to come in and film a battle. From this was produced a fine film called *Dead Birds* that told the story of the Dani tribesmen beautifully and authentically. The missionaries in the valley were furious, for they had been trying to discourage these wars. Then a film company, with the help of the Broekhuyses, allowed a battle to be filmed and later shown to the world.

The missionaries complained bitterly to the government and Jan was fired. The film has rarely been shown to the general public by agreement between the Peabody Museum and the Dutch government. I found a copy by good luck and I have shown it to a number of friends and clubs. I believe the protesters were making a mountain out of a molehill.

One day Jan took us downriver in a motor boat for some duck hunting and a look into one of the villages. To my amazement, I found that none of the natives had developed any sort of boats. Their transport on the water was to stand on a floating log and guide or move it with a paddle. These people were primitive, no doubt about that. Once I saw a man cutting down a tree with a stone ax. Their yam gardens, however, were well-developed and extensive.

The village we visited was on the river's edge and was surrounded by a stone wall, used primarily to keep in the pigs. The women, when they were not working the gardens, spent much of their time in the Long House, cooking and gossiping. The one we entered was dark and smelly. Pigs wandered in and out while children crawled over the dirt floor. The men had their own house where they could get together in daytime, but families got together at night in their own house.

We were finally beginning to appreciate the food

shortage, because many natives approached the patrol post to complain that their gardens were flooded and they had nothing to eat. We noticed our two meals, breakfast and dinner, consisted of bread, cold bacon, and cheese. The nights were cold and we needed three blankets on our beds.

Word reached us at the patrol post that an American missionary couple, Jerry and Darlene Rose, wanted us to join them for Sunday dinner at their mission station at Tulem, some forty-five minutes away by patrol boat. The river was high and we saw many flooded gardens along the way. There was a real threat of famine and Jan was worried. It meant the increased possibility of raiding wars against better supplied villages elsewhere. He hoped that the government would be able to fly rice or some other food substitutes in from Hollandia.

Jerry and Darlene, both Americans, turned out to be two pleasant and industrious people who managed to combine missionary zeal with a successful business sense. They owned a generator and had a large, productive garden with a variety of vegetables. Chickens were scratching about the house. Most of the Europeans at Patrol Post Baliem welcomed an invitation to the Roses'. They didn't serve beer, but their roast chicken was delicious. The Roses had been in New Guinea since 1938, making them real "old New Guinea hands."

The day was clear and pleasant. We sat outside with Jerry and Darlene, watching the clouds drift by, while we exchanged news of the States and stories of early New Guinea. At noon, we were invited inside to join for dinner of roast chicken, mashed potatoes, boiled cabbage, and some other garden succulents. It was a meal I shall never forget.

Jerry had a small staff of native converts working

for him at his church, in his garden, and at his home. He and his wife were living a relatively comfortable and secure life surrounded by people who respected, maybe even revered them. We sat down to the dinner table and I awaited the meal eagerly, for I was very hungry after living on white bread and cheese at the patrol post.

Darlene had prepared the Sunday dinner and it was served to us by her "house boy," to use the term loosely.

He appeared at the table stark naked except for a coating of pig's grease on his body and the usual penis gourd. It kept banging against the tray and interfering with his serving. However, he kept pushing it out of the way with complete aplomb, finally settling on a convenient position between the tray and his bare tummy. When the tray of mashed potatoes finally reached me I couldn't determine whether the smell of hot mashed potatoes and gravy atoned for the smell of sweat and pig's grease--but I was hungry and common sense prevailed.

On our return to Hollandia, I met once again with Jaap Lind and expressed my ultimate desire to join with a patrol on a trek into the unexplored interior of New Guinea. Jaap had just been assigned as the head patrol officer to Post Oebroeb. He invited us to join him there and take me on such a patrol. The temptation was too great and in 1961 Stevey and I took the challenge.

*Chapter Six*

# New Guinea Jungle Patrol

After returning to Los Angeles I began my research into the state of affairs in New Guinea and what problems might have to be faced there—for this was a relatively unknown and unexplored area of the world and the political situation was unsettled.

On January 26, 1962, an article in the *Sydney Morning Herald* of Sydney, Australia, deplored the fact that the border between Australian New Guinea and its neighbor to the west, Dutch New Guinea, was so poorly defined. The Australian government was understandably concerned because Indonesia, by mutual agreement with Holland, was about to take over the administration of all Western New Guinea. At that time, Sukarno was still the dictator of Indonesia, and Australia was justifiably worried that this volatile ruler might try and create an "incident" over this ill-defined border to further enhance his rather shaky position within his own country.

In 1895, Holland and Britain signed a treaty fixing the border as beginning in the south at the mouth of the Bensback River, a natural marker at 141 degrees 1 minute 48 seconds east. This border continued in a straight line north until it met the Fly River, which it followed as it bulged into Dutch territory. Thus, the whole of the Fly River was in the Australian side. It then followed the

141st meridian north. These boundaries remained the same after the Australians took over in 1920, but it was a poor arrangement with the boundary running mainly through inhospitable, almost completely unexplored country covered with heavy jungles and high mountains.

Shortly after Indonesia's takeover, the Australian government began frantic efforts to survey the border and establish control in a number of "enclaves"* that existed in this border region. The enclave area in question was about eighty miles southeast of Hollandia and measured probably thirty-five miles from north to south and an average of ten miles east to west. The area comprised three enclaves: Waris, Waina Sowanda, and Dera. The Dutch thought it was their territory because of confusion over the position of the frontier, the 141st meridian, between Australian and Dutch New Guinea. The access from the Dutch side was easier than it was from the Australian side because of a range of dense jungle mountains intervening. It was not surprising that the Dutch got there first, since the approach from their side was considerably easier.

However, when the mistake was discovered, amicable arrangements were made between the two governments, allowing the Dutch some administrative control over these enclaves. It was hoped that in due time slowly advancing Australian patrols would penetrate the region from their side and eventually establish patrol posts. Then the Dutch would relinquish control of the enclaves to Australia.

It was my good fortune in 1961 to be invited to join a Dutch government patrol that was entering these en-

---

*Enclave. A territory surrounded by another country. In this case Dutch territory surrounded by Australian New Guinea territory.

claves for the purpose of establishing some sort of administrative control over the many primitive tribes of people that inhabited this remote and inhospitable jungle. The patrol consisted of one Dutch officer, several police, a medical orderly, and twelve carriers. It did little more than collect occasional information and administer penicillin shots to the sick who were willing to submit and "show the flag."

This was still largely unexplored jungle with exciting prospects of meeting new and interesting tribes of natives still unaffected and unspoiled by European culture and influence. My purpose was to film the daily life of the patrol and, as much as possible, the way of life of the people we would encounter in the villages on the way. Stevey, accustomed to exploring and hardships, would accompany me on part of this trip.

We finally arrived at Lake Sentani airstrip on September 26, 1961, after a wearisome flight from Lae in an aged DC-3. Lake Sentani is about fifteen miles south of Hollandia and during World War II served as an important American bomber base. I remember it well, having lived for six months in the nearby jungles in 1944.

We were met at the airstrip by Jaap Lind. Lind was the district officer for Oebroeb and would head the patrol we would join to explore the enclaves. Jaap took us by jeep to the Hotel Moorman, an antiquated and smelly claptrap just outside of Hollandia. The first-class government hotel, where I had stayed once before, apparently had no accommodations for Jaap so he rather arbitrarily moved us out and into the Moorman Hotel where we would share his misery. In the afternoon, after we had consumed an awesome lunch of soup and very hot curry, Jaap came by and explained to us in detail the patrol that would take us through the jungles from patrol post Oebroeb to the enclaves. At this point Stevey began to have doubts about undertaking such an arduous journey. We finally agreed that she would fly with us to Oebroeb and stay at the patrol post with Jaap's wife while I accompanied Jaap on patrol.

I spent the entire day in Hollandia shopping at the poorly stocked trade stores, attempting to buy canned food, tobacco, axes, knives, and other goods that would be needed for the patrol. Some of these items would be used for our own purposes, but most would be for trade or "inducements." Most of the carriers, Jaap informed me, would not accept cash for their services, but preferred to be paid in food, tobacco, knives, and other trade items. In the evening, we had dinner with Rene Wassing, a young and very likeable Dutch government anthropologist who was about to leave for the south coast to join Michael Rockefeller who was on a search for native art.*

At last we were off! A Papuan driver drove the three of us in a government Land Rover to Lake Sentani airstrip. Here, after much conversation and the signing of many "no responsibility" documents, we concluded arrangements with the Catholic Mission station for two light Cessnas to fly us and our supplies to Oebroeb. Our pilots were both young Dutchmen who spent most of their time flying to remote missions and government posts with necessary food and medical supplies. After a long delay, we finally took off from Sentani and headed for Oebroeb, which lay in the jungles about one hundred miles southeast of Hollandia. I confess my heart sank when I looked at the rugged jungle terrain below. It would be most impossible for us to cross it on foot.

There appeared to be a few four-thousand-foot peaks.

*Wassing did join Rockefeller on the South Coast where Michael died under mysterious circumstances.

However, the elevation was mostly between fifteen hundred and two thousand feet, and the country was crossed by many large rivers, the land completely covered with gigantic trees, some over 180 feet high. The pilot told us that the rainfall in this area averaged over two hundred inches a year.

Oebroeb appeared as a tiny clearing in a sea of green jungle. It was established in January 1961, and as we made our approach from the air, it looked lonely and forbidding.

When we landed, Jaap's wife, Elen, was there to greet us and help unload the plane. The pilot was anxious to head back for Sentani before low clouds and rain made flying too dangerous. Elen appeared to be a confident and capable young woman. This was fortunate because she was often alone at the post with her two young children while Jaap was away on patrol visiting the territory he administered.

The four government houses at Oebroeb were prefabs with tin roofs and fairly comfortable. All the parts had been flown in, piece by piece. As Stevey was to learn, to her dismay, during a rainstorm the noise on the tin roof was almost unbearable. The huts did not have any electricity or plumbing. Washing had to be done in the nearby river. All supplies had to be flown in by air, including much of the food. The natives in this valley subsisted mainly on a diet of sago palm and a local sweet potato, both not very palatable to most Europeans.

Quarters were under construction for a contingent of police who would eventually be flown in from Hollandia. In the meantime, law and order of the district was in the hands of Jaap Lind.

That evening, in the quiet of our damp, stuffy little room and under our mosquito nets, Stevey and I had a chance to examine our situation. We were now completely isolated from contact with the outside world except by radio and at the mercy of our hosts. Both Jaap and Elen appeared to be fairly interesting people with intelligence. Both were atheists, as they quickly informed us. I suppose they did this to distinguish themselves from the rather typical "missionary" types so often found in these remote jungle outposts.

Days later, when I was reunited with Stevey in Hollandia, she told me that life at Oebroeb while I was gone had been unbearably boring. She and Elen had little in common and most of the books in the house were either French or Dutch. It rained almost continuously, the noise on the tin roof making sleep almost impossible. She worried mainly about whether the rain would ever stop long enough to allow a plane to land and that she might be stuck in Oebroeb forever. I knew she silently cursed me.

The next morning, Jaap insisted that we go for a short practice hike in the "bush" to test our equipment and to see how it would feel to walk after swimming a river and to acquaint us with jungle conditions. It was a dramatic test, and I could see the look of concern on Stevey's face.

Post Oebroeb lay in a low valley with a large, muddy river running its length. It was surrounded by a range of heavily forested mountains. The daytime temperature was oppressively hot and humid, although nights usually brought rain and some cooling.

There were five Europeans living in Oebroeb: Jaap and Elen Lind, their two small children and Father John, a Dutch Catholic priest, who ran a small mission nearby. There were a few natives, mostly trained government employees, who helped run the post. The native population numbered several hundred.

Oebroeb was totally isolated from the outside world except by radio or aircraft. Aircraft were subject to the whims of very tricky weather and an always soggy airstrip. It would take weeks to walk through the jungle to the north coast and the terrain was so rugged that only the most experienced hiker could undertake such a journey. On occasion, heavy rains so inundated the primitive little airstrip that no planes were able to land for weeks. At such times, the food situation became serious, although hardly desperate. Nearby native gardens could always supply some food. In a way, the sense of isolation was rather pleasant. It was almost complete and offered a person a chance to feel dependent only on that which immediately surrounded him.

Jaap had received word through the "jungle grapevine" that a rather rare and unusual dance feast was about to take place at the village of Amgotro, almost seven hours' walking distance from Oebroeb. Jaap believed that Elen and Stevey could manage this trek so plans were being made to employ carriers and pack our supplies. The plan was for the women to walk with us to Amgotro, stay with us there until the dance ceremony was over, then return to Oebroeb by themselves with three carriers and a policeman.

The four of us and our carriers finally made it to Amgotro after seven hours of difficult hiking over jungle trails that were muddy and slippery and crossed with many streams. The last hour of walking was entirely in knee-deep water, and the heat and humidity were oppressive. Most of the time we passed through typical rain forest that smelled rank and rotten. Leeches were in great abundance and seemed to be able to attach themselves to almost any part of our body, despite the fact that we covered ourselves with as much protective clothing as possible. After a few hours on the trail, we were all bleeding from leech-bite wounds. The carriers seemed to suffer the most. They were barefoot and constantly scraping the leeches off their legs. Jaap told me that a leech, when it attaches itself to the skin, injects a noncoagulant into the bloodstream, causing the wound to bleed profusely. There was a considerable amount of blood running from the carriers' legs. It was often possible to follow their trail by the drops of blood on the ground!

Tribal chief—Highlands of Papua New Guinea

Dance of Fertility—Iryan Jaya

Native girls prepare to dance—Malaita Islands, Solomons

The village chief with his two children—Solomon Islands

Preparing the pig feast—Papua New Guinea

A land diver prepares to jump from an eighty foot tower with only vines attached to his ankles to stop his fall—Pentecost Island, Vanuatu

Village woman—Solomon Islands

Two women celebrating the John Fram Cargo Cult—Sulphur Bay, Vanuatu

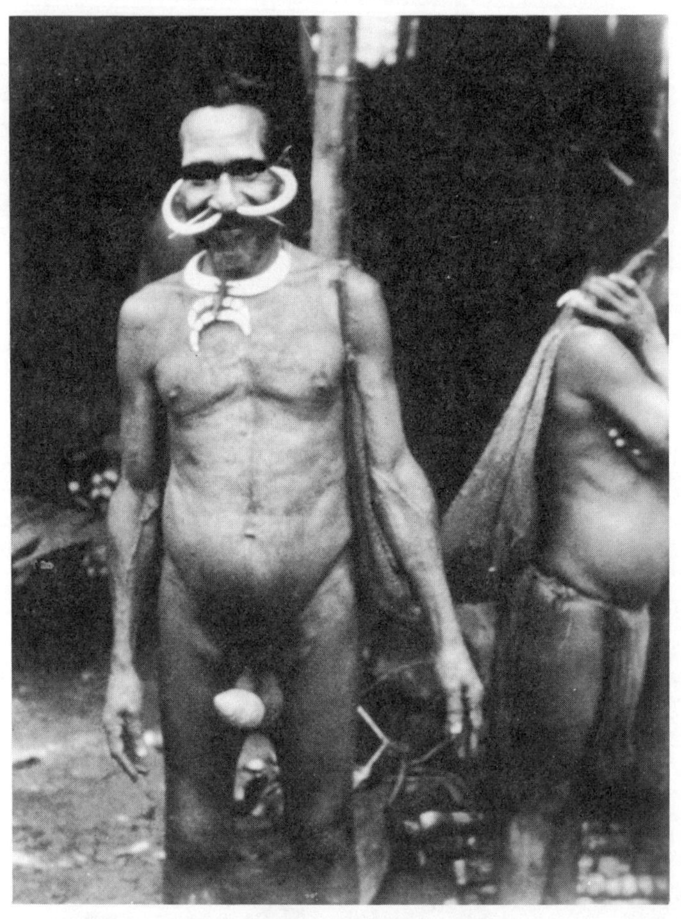

A gourdman of New Guinea wearing his only
clothes, the penis sheath—Iryan Jaya

The land divers prepare for their jumps while the women watch and chant—Pentecost Island, Vanuatu

*Chapter Seven*

# Dance of the Dead

We reached Amgotro in the late afternoon and entered the village unannounced. Surprisingly, our arrival didn't seem to create any unusual interest among the people, except for the curious children. Perhaps the natives resented our intrusion, but no one showed any hostility. Jaap was a Big Man with recognized authority.

Amgotro normally had a population of about two hundred people, a large village for this region. Now it was almost double that number with the many visitors from other villages who had come to take part in the ceremony.

We were directed to a hut, somewhat isolated from Amgotro, which was to be our living quarters during our visit. Actually, it was a *haus kiap** or patrol house that most villages provided for important visitors and government patrol officers. It was a rather dilapidated hut, constructed of split bamboo and elevated about six feet off the ground. We took care to set up our mosquito nets over our cots, for malaria was very prevalent. Our own carriers made their beds under the patrol house. We were a crowded, chummy, smelly lot.

Our carriers, all young men from Oebroeb, seemed

* *Kiap* is the native word for chief.

to prefer not to leave the vicinity of the patrol house and they mixed infrequently, or not at all, with the people of Amgotro. This puzzled me at first. Jaap later told me that this was rather typical behavior in New Guinea. The men from Oebroeb, only a seven-hour walk from Amgotro, felt frightened and as unwelcome strangers in the village.

Tribes of people who have lived in such isolation from one another for so many years and separated by high mountains, dense jungles and swift rivers and a fear of the unknown tend to distrust one another. The men of Oebroeb may well have suspected that the people of Amgotro might be directing evil spirits at them.

The primitive natives of this region of New Guinea were mostly of the Dera tribe, estimated to be about eighteen hundred in number. Physically, most were small in stature, the men averaging a little over five feet in height. They were, by reputation, an enthusiastic, energetic people, but often given to rather violent temperamental explosions. As a consequence, warfare and murder were not uncommon. Suspicion and mistrust of strangers ruled their lives. However, there was no evidence of the practice of cannibalism and headhunting, as found elsewhere in New Guinea.

Men and boys went unclothed, except for the small, round penis gourd. Pierced nose septums usually held pigs' tusks. Often a necklace of shells or tusks was worn. Other than this, little attempt was made at adornment, except on ceremonial occasions. Women and girls all wore the loose-fitting grass skirts (made of the sago fiber) that extended to the knees. They also preferred necklaces of bright shells and glass beads, when these were available.

After spreading our bedrolls and rigging mosquito nets in our *haus kiap*, we laboriously removed the leeches from our legs and arms and enjoyed a bath in the water of a nearby, fast-running stream. One of our carriers prepared dinner by boiling cans of meat and potatoes in a large metal bucket. Considerably refreshed, we gathered our equipment and made our plans to observe and film the preparations for the dance.

We were attracted to one end of the village where a specially constructed "Men's House" buzzed with excitement and activity. Here the men were preparing their costumes for the dance ceremony. All the dancers were from outside the villages. Men of the host village did not participate in the dance itself but helped prepare the costumes, dressed the dancers, and provided the food. Women and girls were forbidden to approach the vicinity of the "Men's House." The young men not actually participating in the dance took great delight in screaming threats at any interloping females bold enough to wander near. Entire families had walked many days to reach Amgotro. The village with a normal population of two hundred was now swollen to about four hundred men, women, and children, badly taxing the primitive housing and almost nonexistent sanitation facilities.

Although there appeared to be some "fixed rules" governing the method of dressing for the dance, a great deal of artistic interpretation was in evidence, with startling results. The usual method of dressing was to blacken the face with pig's grease, painting around the eyes with multicolored stains from various fruits and plants. All the men had pierced nose septums. On this occasion, huge pigs' tusks had been thrust through the nose, giving a most fearsome appearance to the wearer. The entire body was then streaked with various colored clays and the neck adorned with shells and more pigs' tusks.

Many seashells were used for decorative purposes as

well as for bartering. The shells reached the village by way of long established "trade routes" from the coast. Knives were much in evidence and were usually worn strapped to a man's arm by a rattan band. These knives were made from the leg bones of the cassowary bird and appeared to be a very formidable weapon. Most impressive of all were the skillfully designed headdresses, constructed of animal skins, shells, beads, and topped by the magnificent plumage of the King of Saxony Bird of Paradise, as well as many green and yellow leaves.

Evening was fast approaching. The dance was about to begin. The drum beats were louder, more insistent. Men, women, and children added to the excitement and tension by running up and down the center of the village uttering odd grunts and cries and appearing as if they were in a hypnotic trance.

At last we were about to witness the Dance of the Dead, a unique dance-feast held every four to five years by the Dera people to honor their dead, and, in this case, the dead of the village of Amgotro. The bodies, fortunately, had long since been disposed of in the ground. Actually, the time elapsed between performances of this traditional dance of the Dera tribe was quite arbitrary and may have depended a great deal upon the number of dead whose "spirits" had to be honored and whether enough food had been collected. Perhaps an even more important reason for the timing of the dance was the condition of the gardens around the village. In this hot, rainy climate, the soil becomes unproductive rapidly, making it necessary to relocate the village to better land. Tradition dictated that once the dance was completed the village was abandoned and put to the torch.

A large group of women had stationed themselves at the entrance to the village, directly in the path the dancers would take. They were wailing and uttering mournful grunts and cries while swinging their sago fiber grass skirts in a curious hip motion. All the women were barebreasted and the children naked, modesty not being of concern to these people.

Then, preceded by barking dogs, a few drummers and a group of frantically excited villagers, the massed dancers, four abreast and about fifty strong, entered the village, moving in slow, rhythmic steps. Upon reaching a large open square located between rows of huts, the dancers in their brilliant and gaudy costumes proceeded in a slow, plodding "figure eight" pattern around the square accompanied by the bizarre noise and confusion of massed drumbeats, shouts, and cries.

This dance represented a very important religious ceremony to the Dera people. Although the Dera do not have a concept of a supreme being as we know it, they did have a mystical belief in semi-gods and idols with totemistic motifs prevailing. The most extensive form of religion found in New Guinea was among those tribes living near ample food supplies and sago, possibly because they had found more spare time and greater opportunity to develop cultural forms. Magic and sorcery played an important part in their spiritual life and they believed that death, except that of very old persons, was the inimical action by wizards or a curse placed by an enemy.

The deep jungle night had settled on Amgotro. By the light of many cooking fires, the dancers continued their same monotonous and unbroken steps around and around the village square. The only musical accompaniment was a dozen drummers hidden behind a bamboo enclosure, pounding out a rhythmic step on their three-foot long instruments, the drum heads covered with snake skins.

As the long night passed, the exhausted dancers occasionally paused to rest and gorge themselves upon roast pig, sugar cane, potatoes, and sago. At such times, their places were taken by new "teams" of dancers so there was no pause in the continuity of the ceremony.

As the light of dawn touched the treetops, we struggled out of our mosquito nets and returned to the village to find that the activities were continuing as before. Groups of women and children sat huddled by their huts watching the ceremony with placid interest while munching on sugar cane. The villagers and dancers of Amgotro still continued to ignore us as we wandered about.

They continued on through the morning hours with the ceremony, although the oppressive heat began to turn the atmosphere into a stifling sweat box. It did not appear that the dancing men were using any drugs or alcohol to fortify themselves during this exhausting ordeal, but I became aware of an almost "dreamlike" sensation induced by my own fatigue, the monotonous drumbeats, and the sheer power of the dance.

Feasting was uninterrupted. The women had prepared great quantities of sago, a favorite food of the Dera people. To us it was a tasteless, gummy, unpalatable mess. Sago is made from the fibrous center of the sago palm tree. The fiber is ground into a pulp and mixed with hot water to become a paste. The abundance of sago palms in this area made the procurement of food a relatively simple matter. Many pigs had been slaughtered a few days earlier in a ritualistic and bloody chase that allowed the pigs to run wild through the village until they were either speared or arrowed to death by the men and boys. Pig's meat, or any meat, is rare in New Guinea and usually eaten only on festive occasions. The Dera people maintained a largely vegetarian diet except once or twice a year when they gorged themselves on pig's meat during celebrations.

Sometime during the early afternoon, we noticed that dance activities had come almost to a halt. Most of the men had disappeared into the men's house, where they were preparing and putting on new and more elaborate costumes for a new phase of the ceremony. At about this time, an older and highly respected warrior and hunter of the village was running wildly about, firing arrows in "near misses" at the hordes of small boys gathered about. The boys, in turn, ran screaming and shrieking in every direction in mock terror of the fate that might befall them. This ritual, the Dera people believed, would impart courage and bravery to their young men and help them to grow up to be fearless hunters and warriors.

The drummers began to increase the volume and tempo of their drumbeats to a thudding, brain-rattling crescendo. Suddenly, about thirty to forty dancers burst from the men's house and whirled into the village square, running and gyrating about in undisciplined but graceful spins and leaps. At that point a number of men, women, and children who previously had taken no active part in the dancing, leaped from the sidelines, grasped hold of the grass skirts of the dancers and pranced after them. Those who joined the "spirit" dancers were relatives of the deceased. To show their respect and to honor their dead, they cried and shouted words of praise. These newly costumed men were the spirit dancers and each represented the spirit of a person of Amgotro who had died during the previous four or five years. The new dance dress had a three- or four-foot headdress of antenna-like construction, made of bamboo and topped by jungle leaves and flowers. The faces and bodies of the dancers were completely covered to the knees by long grass and leaves, with only narrow openings at eye level. It was hard to believe that these men, having danced almost continuously for twenty-four hours, could leap and whirl about as they did. Their headdresses must have weighed twenty or thirty pounds. Their bodies were covered with a thick coat of *kunae* grass. In the steamy heat of the New Guinea jungle it seemed almost physically impossible.

As the afternoon light began to fade away, the still madly whirling dancers and their supporters gradually began to congregate and dance directly in front of the bamboo enclosure, which had hidden the drummers throughout the two days and night. In the dim light and at some signal, the people of Amgotro began tearing away the enclosure, while the drummers, in their bright textile headdresses, beads and shells, approached the center of the village square. All sound ceased in the village of Amgotro, while the drummers knelt in silence. An elder of the village approached in the gloom with a large stick held high above his head. With a quick snap, the stick was broken in two. The drummers and dancers suddenly leaped to their feet in a final, furious burst of activity. The symbolic breaking of the stick had "released" the spirits of the dead from their human bodies forever. The Dance of the Dead was over; the weary villagers lapsed into a night of feasting and exhausted sleep.

On the following morning, while our carriers packed gear for the long trek north, we watched tired groups of visitors collect their few meager belongings and whatever food was still left, preparing for the journey home. The people of Amgotro were also packing, for they were about to abandon their village and put it to the torch. To remain in Amgotro now would only encourage the "spirits" of the dead to return and haunt them. So, all earthly reminders would be destroyed by flame.

*Chapter Eight*

# Into the Unknown

Stevey, Elen, and their carriers departed in the morning for their trek back to Oebroeb. Stevey looked depressed and worried, fearing she might never see me again.

Jaap was in a great state of agitation. Most of our carriers had disappeared during the night and made their way back to Oebroeb. They had not yet been paid for their services, so their fear of the Dera must have been very real. Who knows what threats they might have heard? Jaap believed that these superstitious men were frightened that some village witch doctor had "hexed" the trail they were about to set out on. Perhaps they had second thoughts about continuing on into unfriendly country amidst strange people. We could sense the fear in our few remaining carriers.

By mid-morning Jaap succeeded in hiring other men to replace the ones who had run away. Assembled and loaded, we started out for the village of Kamando, which we had to reach in order to find a place to sleep.

The trek took ten hours and remains indelibly printed in my memory for life. Up and down steep ridges, slipping, sliding, falling, always in ankle deep mud. The heat and humidity was overpowering. The damp, dark jungle pressed in on all sides. I felt I was walking in a narrow tunnel. The silence was eerie, only occasionally broken by the thrashing wings of the giant hornbills as they fled to safety from our noisy column of men. Shallow streams offered easy paths with the least resistance. We would follow them, sloshing along in the cool water.

Sometime during the day the patrol reached the Poe River. There was no bridge. It was too deep to do anything but swim across. This operation took nearly an hour. First, we had to locate long vines that were strung across the river to act as a "safety line" to keep the swift current from sweeping us away. The water was muddy and treacherous looking. I preferred not to think about the crocs lurking there.

Our equipment had to be repacked to prevent it from getting wet. We built a small raft and floated my camera and film across. I had already packed them in watertight cans but had they fallen into the river that would have been the end of my filming endeavors.

After this difficult and time-consuming experience, we walked until nightfall. At this point we became separated from the bulk of our carriers. Jaap concluded that they had decided to sleep on the trail. So, we pushed on.

It was hard enough in the daytime, but to manage the trail at night was folly, a nightmare of falls. Jaap had one Coleman lantern and several flashlights. Mud and rain had turned the trail into a quagmire. Occasionally, we stopped long enough to remove the leeches from our legs, arms, faces, and heads, but did not stop long enough to eat. Jaap's policy was that once on the trail one must never stop to eat, even if it meant going ten hours without food.

We finally struggled into the tiny village of Kamando late at night. The village had the usual *haus kiap*. I staggered in and flopped on the dirt floor with my wet clothes and fell promptly to sleep, not waking until morning. Someone had thoughtfully removed my boots during the night.

In the morning, all of our carriers showed up at the village, but many refused to go any further with us, despite Jaap's threats and pleadings. Definitely a "hex" had been placed on the trail.

After lengthy palavering, we managed to recruit new carriers from the village of Kamando, but only after Jaap brought out inducements of strong, black tobacco, steel axes, and promises of other goodies tucked away in our supplies.

It was another day of the usual climbing, sliding, slipping and falling, always in heavy mud. The jungle was so thick that it was rarely possible to see the sun; I was soon soaked with perspiration from head to foot. The leeches were not so prevalent, perhaps because it was a rarely traveled trail. We made five river crossings on this day, fortunately none was deeper than our necks. I marveled at the carriers' ability to keep their footing in the swift waters. We all used a stout pole to keep our balance.

The carrier line would sometimes spread out over a distance of half a mile. Occasionally, to frighten away evil spirits, the carriers would break into a curious, prolonged eerie whooping noise, probably to keep in contact with the others.

On one occasion we got lost and had to spend agonizing hours retracing the trail and cursing our guides. Once, while pulling myself up a steep incline, I reached to grab the closest support available. It was a nettlebush, and for a few hours my arm was swollen and painful.

Toward evening, we reached a small village called Wijala. About fifty families lived here, working their nearby potato gardens and hunting for the few small rats, marsupials, and birds of the jungle. It was a sparse life and the people showed it. Jaap had patrolled through this village before and the natives were familiar with him. We were treated with friendly curiosity but allowed no privacy throughout the day or night. Our every action was observed with intense interest.

Although my calendar was dated October 3, time had lost all meaning. We finally got away from Wijala, but only after going through the same routine of recruiting new carriers.

The jungle was becoming more mountainous now and we were forced to endure steep climbs, usually in heavy rain. It was dark and difficult to see.

Another hazard were the wild pig traps along the trail, covered with brush. A careless step would cause one to fall through onto bamboo spears embedded in the bottom of the trap. These traps were easy enough to avoid if one knew what to watch out for—but I did not, because my glasses were fogged.

On occasion we found ourselves walking along the top of knifelike ridges that would fall off almost straight down for six hundred to eight hundred feet. A fall here would certainly have caused serious injury. It would be a difficult task aiding a person out of this region.

We carried our food with us and ate only twice a day—breakfast and dinner. In the morning, our diet consisted of dried biscuits with cheese or sugar. We consumed great quantities of tea or coffee with vast amounts of sugar added. At night we would heat cans of food, usually meat and potatoes, and eat them out of the can with spoons.

On a few occasions, we supplemented our diet with native potatoes and other vegetables and fruits, which we bought in the villages, when available. The carriers' principal diet seemed to consist of sago,* bananas, and potatoes.

---

* The fibrous center of the sago palm tree, ground and mixed with boiling water.

All the natives that we met, both men and women, smoked constantly, using a locally grown tobacco leaf that they rolled into cigars. I tried a few but found them bitter.

The villages along the trail were small and infrequent, but whenever we arrived we always had a hut to sleep in. Usually we shared space with our carriers if there was room; if not, those who could not get in slept under the hut, which was elevated several feet off the ground.

Jaap and I both slept in our shorts and on air mattresses with mosquito nets rigged above us. We were trekking at an elevation of about fifteen hundred feet. The weather was constantly hot.

At night, in many of the villages, the native men would crowd into the hut we occupied and sit around staring at us, talking excitedly among themselves. I had no sense of fear, although I know our carriers did. To these people, Jaap and I were the honored, protected white men who represented some unknown but recognized authority from far away, but our carriers were just some troublemakers from another tribe.

When Jaap would turn on his radio, the excitement became intense. The men would shout, laugh, and push each other in great hilarity. I felt like a Hollywood celebrity as I was eyed with intense curiosity. It never once occurred to me that these people might harm me.

When I dozed off to sleep I noticed that the villagers, as many as could do so, simply remained in the hut and slept the night with us. Their body odors were strong and offensive, probably because of the pigs' grease and the lack of bathing. All the villages were built on high ridges for protection against raiders and to get down to the river was an arduous and time-consuming task. The job of water collecting was usually assigned to the women, the water carried in cleverly designed palm leaf buckets.

The last hour of our walk from Wijala to Nei was almost straight up in heavy mud and rain. At the top of the ridge was the most spectacular sight. Off in the distance rose the Waria mountains, about four thousand feet in elevation. In between was ridge after ridge of dense, forbidding jungle. It looked so uninhabited and impenetrable. I now knew why the Australians left it alone.

As our patrol approached the village of Nei, after a long climb, the men streamed out to meet us, apparently aware for some time that we were arriving. The natives greeting us were short in stature, probably about five feet tall. They wore no clothing, except the usual small round gourd attached to the end of their penises. Their hair was black and kinky, their skin a chocolate brown. Their physiques were slim and muscular.

Jaap used an interpreter to converse, who translated the local language into Malay, which Jaap understood. There was little of the conversation comprehended except when Jaap deigned to let me know, which was not often.

After a dinner of meat and potatoes with hot coffee, we retired to our *haus kiap* when night fell. Every man in the village who could, crowded in. We rarely saw women. Jaap turned on his shortwave radio and created an instant sensation. Every sound coming from the "box" was greeted with howls of laughter and shouted exclamations, and Jaap, playing on his popularity, would switch from station to station. I have never seen men so attentive and exhilarated.

Exhausted and wet as I was, I enjoyed the show. Some time after midnight, I dozed off and my last memory was of a ring of curious men seated in rapt attention around the radio. When I awoke in the morning, they were still there.

My relationship with Jaap was beginning to deteriorate. I realized now why he had put himself out in this "bush" job and isolated himself from the rest of the world. Jaap was a nonconformist, a man angry at the rest of the world. He had a love/hate attitude toward Americans, whom he respected as the world's best businessmen but the world's greediest capitalists. He preferred to talk about cars, if he talked to me at all. At this point we scarcely spoke to each other, both of us burying ourselves in our private thoughts.

I set up my movie camera in the village and began filming. At first there was no sign of any women. When I asked, the men ordered them out of the huts to be photographed. They were shy and nervous about my activities.

Unfortunately, except for the very young girls, most of the women were singularly unattractive. Their hair was braided and greasy, their breasts huge and sagging, their stomachs terribly distended, either as the result of pregnancy or from the high starch diet.

Malaria was prevalent among the villagers, and malnutrition was obvious. In addition, frambesia (a form of yaws) was common and almost everyone seemed to have suppurating sores on their legs. Mosquitoes were in great abundance, but I quickly learned to avoid scratching bites as much as possible, because infection set in too quickly.

While I was filming, our Hollandia-trained medical assistant set up a first aid station and treated as many of the people as wished to be taken care of. Since many of them had seen the good results of the doctor's previous visit, few were reluctant. I got a shot of penicillin for my infected cuts.

The women in most of the villages that we had so far visited appeared to do all of the cooking, tended the children, and looked after the gardens—although men would usually join in the heavy work of cultivating the gardens.

The men hunted wild pigs, birds, rats, and marsupials, using bows and arrows as weapons.

The native men seemed to love to sit around, chatting and joking and discussing village affairs. Jaap had heard of instances of a considerable amount of tribal warfare, ambushes and murder, but had not been able to determine, so far, whether these people practiced cannibalism or headhunting. The men of the village denied any such practice, but they were also vaguely aware of the "White Man's Law" that punished people for such crimes.

It was now October 5. We headed off to the village of Oemeda, about a four-hour walk. Nothing existed between these tiny settlements but jungle and occasional openings where a potato garden had been prepared. At one time we came across a group of hunters looking for wild game. They were frightened by us and ran away.

Most of the time I just slogged ahead, sometimes getting lost, sweating and cursing the miserable jungle and depending more and more on my stout pole to keep my balance. Jaap, as usual, was flying ahead, berating the carriers, trying to prove his manhood.

Our daily routine each morning was to listen to the shortwave radio and the various patrol posts calling in to Hollandia. These posts usually stated the weather conditions, their various needs, and other pertinent information. It was all in Dutch so I understood only what Jaap told me.

My boots, bought just before I left, were in the early stages of disintegration. One heel had fallen off and a village dog had gotten into the hut and chewed the tops off. Obviously, as Jaap informed me, I had bought inferior American equipment. The toenails of my right foot were beginning to fall off. Without an extra pair of boots, I knew I was in trouble.

Our patrol trekked on to Oemeda, reaching there sometime in the late afternoon. Most of the villages we had passed through were small, with no more than twenty to thirty people. Sanitary conditions were poor and the people did not seem to be concerned with washing themselves. This may have been for several reasons; the villages were built on high ground and getting down to the river must have been difficult. The rivers were muddy and ran swiftly. Drowning would be easy. There were crocodiles along the banks and they always presented a hazard.

At the village of Oemeda, I spent the better part of an hour getting a woman to build a fire outside her hut in order that I might film the preparation of sago, staple of the native diet. Sago is the fibrous center of the sago palm tree. The tree is cut down and split open, then the center of the tree gouged out. The fibrous material is then pounded by the women until it becomes a very coarse white powder. To cook the sago, the fire is built and stones are placed in the fire. When the stones are hot, they are placed in a palm leaf bucket filled with water, which quickly comes to a boil. The boiling water is then poured into a bucket of sago and thoroughly mixed by hand. The sago, after cooling, congeals into a gooey mass, which is wrapped in banana leaves and stored for future use.

We went barefoot around the villages in order that our boots might dry out. I found it much easier to keep my footing without shoes because we were constantly fighting mud. Each night, I faithfully dried out my silica gel, cleaned and dried the camera equipment. I was fearful that fungus might get to the exposed film and lenses. It was almost impossible to have dry clothing to wear at any time. It was so moist and humid and rainy that nothing dried. During the day all our clothing had to be packed for travel. The practical answer would have been to wear only boots and shorts, as Jaap often did.

Our next trek was from Oemeda to the village of Pouenda, another half day over slippery jungle trails. The moment we entered Pouenda the people looked "different." Physically, the men were much the same as those in the other villages we had passed through. However, they grew their hair longer, braided it, and rubbed it in pigs' grease. They were less friendly and came out to meet us armed to the teeth with spears and bows and arrows. I could not tell if we were welcome. Our carriers were frightened out of their wits. Jaap put on a bold front and led the patrol into the village as if he owned it.

The men were costumed as usual with the now familiar penis gourd and the pigs' tusks through the septum of the nose. However, the men were never without their spears and always seemed to be ready to go on the hunt— or was it the warpath?

Jaap had offered a few "inducement goods" and persuaded the men of the village to perform their "Fertility Dance" in order that I might make a film record of it. Actually, this dance was performed formally only on rare occasions and supposedly often ended in mass sex orgies, the men raping any women they could catch. Since this was only a rehearsal, nothing could be confirmed. I tended to believe the story when I witnessed the dance.

A considerable amount of preparation had gone into dressing for the dance. Only the heads of the dancers were decorated—with flowers, leaves, and the beautiful bird of paradise feathers. The men's bodies were naked but painted with clay, and pigs' tusks were worn through their septums.

Now, a much larger gourd was placed on the penis, which was filled with small pebbles to produce a rattling effect. Bows and arrows were carried by the men and often aimed at us in a threatening manner. The "orchestra" was about a dozen men, some beating on drums, others blowing on wood horns, which produced a dull booming sound. The dance consisted of the performers doing a series of wild gyrations and prancings, done in line, with the men using a grinding hip motion that swung their gourds back and forth between their legs. All of this was done in the center of the village with the women well out of sight.

After the dance ended, we passed out tobacco and salt and spent a good many hours gathering what information we could about local customs, types of weapons used, animals hunted, et cetera. However, the attitude of the men seemed reserved and slightly hostile, and our carriers were nervous and anxious to leave, fearing an attack. We carried no weapons and would have been helpless.

With some trepidation, we spent the night in the village, having no other choice. It passed without incident. The sounds in the morning when we awoke were magnificent. Every conceivable jungle bird must have been singing or calling. It was truly a wonderful symphony.

My dressing was done with utmost care, following Jaap's example. First I put on two pairs of long socks, which unfortunately were always wet. Then came long pants and shirt, also wet. Boots were put on last since they needed the greatest chance to dry.

Next it was necessary to check out my equipment. I filled my canteen with tea, heavily laden with sugar for energy. I had to be certain my walking stick was available, for it was an absolute necessity while fording streams and negotiating steep trails. I would then check my camera equipment to make certain that the camera was dry, loaded for action, and securely wrapped.

The next step was to get our medic to attend to our

many cuts and infections. By this time, Jaap was getting the carriers organized, because they would do nothing until urged on two or three times. However, once under way, they were willing, strong walkers and they climbed and descended the precipitous trails easily.

Finally, everything prepared, we slowly wound our way out of the village and into the jungle darkness. By now we had added more carriers to our line because Jaap was trying to collect native artifacts for the museum in Hollandia: drums, stone axes, gourds, and headdresses. I was anxiously hoping that I might be able to keep some for my own collection, which I eventually did.

The natives of this area made an armor that was woven out of a stiff bamboo fiber and designed so that it would pull over the body and protect the wearer's torso from the hip to just under the chin, and high enough in back to cover the neck. It appeared strong enough to stop most spears and arrows, but must have been extremely uncomfortable and restrictive.

Jaap knew that warfare was very traditional among these people. Prearranged battles often took place but sometimes raids were conducted against other villages to steal pigs or women. These were always of a surprise nature. The Dutch and Australian governments were determined to suppress these wars and raids, and occasionally would send in armed patrols to arrest those natives believed guilty of killings.

However, in the area we were exploring, the Dutch and Australian governments had decided that the logistics of such operations were impossible and chose to largely ignore the dozen or more killings that Jaap reported every year. Besides, as Jaap put it, "That's their business, not mine." We carried no weapons. I questioned Jaap as to why. He replied, "This is their country. I have no grudge against these people and if they want to kill me, let them do so."

Jaap was a difficult man. He was big, strong, and arrogant. He was a freethinker and often acted contrary to his government's instructions in dealing with the natives. He hated the missionaries and felt that they were destroying the native cultures to further their own church dogmas.

It was now October 8, and we had been on patrol for nine days. It was either too hot or too wet, or both. My legs were beginning to fester. All of us were constantly stopping to remove the leeches from our arms and legs. No amount of protection seemed to help us. The natives did not seem to bother. They would just scrape them off with a knife. I am sure their tolerance for infection was much higher than mine.

We were on the trail to the village of Kinda, walking in ankle-deep streams. I sweated so profusely that I could not wear my glasses and sometimes stumbled along the trail like a drunken sailor. I smelled so badly that I could not stand myself. Physically, I was beginning to tire, but the mere thought of Jaap watching me pushed me on. I often did not bother swallowing the morning ration of dried biscuits.

Our patrol reached Kinda sometime in the early afternoon and we found it almost deserted, attended by only three old men and a woman. We were told that the other women were out tending their gardens and the men were hunting—or was it raiding?

At Kinda we had our first contact from Oebroeb since leaving on patrol. It seemed their radio had been "out" for a week. We could hear Oebroeb calling Hollandia for supplies and complaining of the constant rains. No aircraft from Hollandia had been able to reach Oebroeb because of the bad weather. Jaap told me that they had often been isolated for a month this way. I could only imagine Stevey's boredom and frustration back at the patrol post. Jaap's radio was getting weaker and soon would be of no further use.

Kinda seemed to be of little interest so we paused only briefly before heading on to the village of Waina, which was about six hours away. Twice, on the trail, our patrol (now consisting of twenty carriers) had to cross deep, swift rivers. To do this, it was necessary to walk across huge logs that had been felled and lay across the river. It required steady, careful negotiating on the wet, slippery surface of the logs to keep balance, and I did not relish contemplating the results if any of us were to fall off. The current was swift, and a man could have been swept out of sight in seconds.

At another river crossing, there was no log and we were forced to swim against a strong, muddy current. We were apprehensive because we knew crocs were in the river. However, we had no accidents. Jaap told me that on occasion when he had been on patrol some rivers had been so swollen and dangerous he made camp and waited for the waters to recede. This would sometimes take many days.

We were lucky! There had not been much rain and the big rivers were not in flood stage. We reached Waina by nightfall. Jaap informed me that we were still in Australian territory, even though at this point he was actually displaying the Dutch flag!

Waina was a very ordinary sort of village and most of the natives wore some sort of clothing. There was even a small mission school with a young native teacher brought in from Hollandia. We had two surprises when we arrived. The schoolteacher had the pupils greet us with a Dutch flag, and they sang the Dutch national anthem!

Another patrol from Waris had walked in to meet us with food, tobacco, salt, and other trade goods. At this point we were penniless, and these items would be used to pay off our carriers, most of whom were from the Waina tribe and were anxious to return home. Salt and steel axes were in the greatest demand and carriers were sorely tempted to work when these were offered.

It was now October 9. The patrol had to push on. The next village to reach would be Sach. Jaap estimated about eight hours of walking; it was a nightmarish struggle. As we prepared ourselves in the morning for the trek, a tremendous rainstorm with thunder and lightning hit us. During the nights, my boots had all but disintegrated and both heels had fallen off. I was forced to borrow a pair from Jaap who enjoyed grumbling about "shoddy American equipment."

We delayed our start, hoping that the rain would let up, but it never did so we pushed off anyway. The rain had turned the trail into a quagmire and it became a truly serious effort to stand up. Everyone, even the carriers, was falling. In the dark, the crashing thunder and lightning flashes were frightening.

Toward the end of the day, we reached the small village where we intended spending the night because the foul weather was making the trail almost impassable. The village was deserted except for two old people who had no intention of moving to the new village site and preferred to die there.

Our patrol, now twenty carriers, two patrol officers, one medic, and myself, moved in and took over the village. Jaap and I found an empty hut, moved in, and knocked out one wall to give us some cross ventilation. We were soaking wet, tired, and hungry. One of the boys got a fire started. Soon we had a good meal of canned meat. I was feeling much encouraged because I knew we should reach the patrol post at Kenandega by next day.

This was our last day on the trail. It was still raining buckets and the trail was treacherous. We reached the Keroom River at noon and forded it with difficulty. It was only waist deep, but very swift. We almost had a fatality when one of the carriers lost his footing and was swept out of sight. We finally found him down the river, battered and bruised, sitting on a sand bar. Several valuable drums and artifacts were lost, as well as some food, but fortunately my camera equipment continued to survive the worst hazards.

After the river crossing, it was but one hour's walk to Kenandega along a good trail with clearing weather. I felt encouraged and strong once again and dreamed of a hot bath, a cold beer, some dry clothes, and a soft bed, as I stumbled the final miles.

Curiously, the native carriers with us, who up to this point had gone naked, stopped and put on shorts but left the pants unzipped with their penis gourds hanging out!

Kenandega was an established Dutch patrol post with an airstrip, police boys, a radio station, and mission school. Here, I knew, eventually a plane would land and fly me back to Hollandia. Fortunately, I discovered that the Catholic priest did have a cold beer, and I thoroughly enjoyed it while Jaap and the Dutch priest argued about the white man's place in darkest New Guinea. The patrol into the Waina enclave had ended and the adventure was over.

When I arrived back in Hollandia, Stevey was waiting for me at the government hotel. The weather at Oebroeb had given her a break and she had managed to fly out the day before. She did not greet me eagerly as her returning hero. I could understand why. I was reminded of a famous quote by some renowned explorer who said, "An adventurer is an explorer who has made a mistake."

Dr. Gallis had made arrangements to fly us to the south coast and visit the Asmat region. By this time my legs were ulcerating. I pleaded ill health and the trip was canceled. This may have been one of the most fortunate pieces of "bad luck" I would ever have. There is little doubt in my mind that once in the Asmat we would have joined up with our friend Rene Wassing, the resident anthropologist in Hollandia, and Mike Rockefeller, son of Nelson Rockefeller, the governor of New York. In all probability they would have invited us to join them on their thirty-foot catamaran to search for wood carvings made by the natives in villages along the coast. It was here that Mike lost his life in a tragic series of events that still remain as mysterious as the disappearance of Amelia Earhart.

Today in New Guinea "old hands" will recite many versions of what really happened to Mike. He drowned; he was eaten by crocs; he's a "white king" living in splendor in some remote mountain village or, as is most generally believed, he was captured by natives and eaten. I wrote Rene Wassing for his version. He replied, "I don't believe that Mike could have ever made it to shore. He must have drowned."

This much is known, Rene and Mike were sailing their catamaran powered by a single outboard motor. The boat was heavily laden with trade goods plus two native helpers. As they passed the mouth of the Eiladen River, a wave swamped the single motor, putting the catamaran at the mercy of the strong currents. The helpless boat was swept out to sea. After a short while, the two natives jumped overboard and swam for shore, three or four miles away.

Rene and Mike stayed with the catamaran while it slowly drifted further out to sea. Good judgment would have dictated sticking with the boat as the two natives would have eventually alerted someone. Mike's impatience got the best of him, and he finally announced to Rene that he was going to "go for it." Rene had no choice but to stay. He could not swim. Rockefeller took the precaution of making "water wings" out of two jerry cans. Once ready, he bid Rene farewell and jumped in. Rene watched him struggling toward the shore, still fighting the currents. He was the last man to see Mike alive. Or was he?

A patrol boat picked up Rene the following morning. He was still clinging to the half-swamped canoe. A ten-day search was conducted by the Dutch using patrol boats and planes. Governor Rockefeller arrived with Michael's twin sister. The search was to no avail, and the Rockefellers left for home. It was generally concluded that Mike must have drowned.

About a week after the search was concluded, Father Kenssel, a Catholic priest living in the area, had a disturbing note from a Dr. Dresser, who was a medical missionary working in Asmat. The note was not very explicit. It stated that there was a possibility that Mike had made it to shore and had been killed by the natives. To this day, no one really knows whatever happened to Mike Rockefeller.

*Chapter Nine*

# Cargo Cults

While exploring the South Seas, I occasionally heard rumors of Cargo Cults. It was told that the natives would go into periods of "madness," uproot their gardens, kill all pigs, even destroy homes. Then, they would build mock ships and airplanes and await the arrival of the cargo they expected to come.

What was the reason for this destructive self-punishment? Messianic religious cults usually tend toward one or two solutions to their disappointment and frustrations—either a return to the Golden Past or the seeking of a New Future. The South Sea Islanders witnessed a vast influx of Europeans, starting as early as the nineteenth century and culminating with the arrival of the armies of Japan, Great Britain, Australia, and America in 1942.

The wealth of goods that the Europeans introduced to the South Seas during those years impressed the natives. However, they were not prepared to understand where it all came from and why it seemed to be bypassing them.

European traders had no real interest in the islands or the people and, with few exceptions, exploited them and left with no regrets on either side. Few islanders ran their own businesses and so had no understanding of com-

merce. Ships would come and discharge cargo for the
white man.

When the missionaries arrived, they tried to impose
European culture on a Melanesian people. The missions
denounced ancient customs, taught the natives false modesty, frowned on dancing, kava drinking and most forms
of pleasure, and superimposed European ideas of Sunday
School, picnics, Mother Hubbard dresses, and hymns in-
stead of their own custom dances and chants. Land was
confiscated in the name of the mission trusts and those
who would not join the mission were banished from their
tribal lands. Early missionaries requested and were given
support by British warships, even to the extent of the
natives being bombarded. The pride, dignity, and customs
of the people were destroyed—they had no one to turn to.
So a visionary's word fell on fertile ground.

Cargo cults have appeared, flourished, and died for
years in the South Seas. They have been and still are
prevalent in New Guinea, Fiji, the Solomon Islands, and
Vanuatu. As long ago as 1919 in Papua New Guinea, the
Vailala Madness was a particularly destructive, antiwhite
cult. Today, on Tanna Island, Vanuatu, many people believe in the John Frum cult. I found myself recreating
the birth of the Cargo Cult as follows:

"All morning long, the people of the village flocked
down to the shores of the lagoon to view the huge ship
in the bay. Its great white sails flapped gently in the
offshore breeze. Some of the braver warriors of the village
leaped into their canoes and rowed out to investigate,
more as an act of bravado than true courage. Rumors had
spread throughout the islands before of great white ships
plying the waters around Malaita, but now, for the first
time, one of the ships had arrived. Mamaluke, sitting
under the shade of a banyan tree, told her sister, 'See, I

told you so; my husband is not afraid, for he dares to go see the Great White Ship.' A few hours later the warriors returned, their canoes laden with sparkling beads, bright cloths, and dazzling gold and silver ornaments. Gina, Mamaluke's husband, exclaimed, 'Look! I have brought all of you these beads and ornaments. In return, I gave them some water, yams, and a few breadfruit. Are we not clever with these strangers?'

"A few hours later, men from the ship rowed to shore in their own dinghy, again bringing more brilliant beads and colorful cloths. These strange men had white skin, blond hair and beards, and wore the most colorful clothing and strange garments on their feet.

"Days passed and these strange, white-skinned men continued to come ashore bringing gifts and taking food in return. At night, they joined in the dances and sang, meanwhile drinking the 'fire water' from their bottles. This 'fire water' did strange things to these men. They tore off their clothes and chased the women and desecrated the sacred grounds of the village. That night Gina spoke to his village council and said, 'These white men are human like us, but evil and they are controlled by a powerful god whom we do not know. What they bring to our village belongs to us. Why else would they be here? This is what our gods prophesied. but their gods are more powerful than ours and we have offended ours by forgetting our sacred obligations to them.'

"The Great White Ship finally left, leaving the people of the village excited with wild images of a strange and powerful world beyond theirs and also a sense of frustration and bewilderment. The goods that the white man had brought in his ships must also belong to them, for it belonged to their world as well, but there was no way they were able to possess all these wonderful things.

As the years went by, the white men and their ships began to ply the islands of the South Seas more and more, and the native people began to realize that none of the cargo in the ships belonged to them. The white man was often brutal, lazy, and demanding. He ordered that they wear his clothing, told them how to worship his god, and made them pay taxes on their own land. Little wonder that an unhappy and frustrated people sought answers from beyond mortal powers. Such was the beginning of the cargo cults in the South Seas.

A very prominent feature of primitive religious experience continues to assert itself in the reconciliation of conflicting beliefs. The leaders of Melanesian cargo cults and other millennium* movements had revealed to them forms of self-denial considered necessary for a new, more satisfying way of life. In cargo cults, this often takes the extreme form of destruction of traditional forms of wealth. The objective of such discipline is to acquire a deeper insight into spiritual reality and lift the person to a state of being that partakes in the divine transcendence.

Messianic movements are usually movements with a marked utopian-revolutionary character. Basic to messianism is a relationship to the time dimension; the time process is expected to lead to major changes, resulting in a happier or more perfect state. The new age might be something new or a return to the golden past. Messianism tends to develop in situations of stress, suffering, or frustration.

A good example of such a condition existed in California in the 1870s. The surviving Indians of the central and northern part of the state participated in a so-called

---

* Millennium: The one thousand years mentioned in the Book of Revelations during which holiness is to be triumphant. Some believe that during this period Christ will reign on earth.

Ghost Dance cult. During the previous twenty years, their frontier had been invaded by prospectors seeking gold. Brawling, murder, disease, polluted streams, destruction of game animals, and fenced-in lands left the native Indians without occupations and ruined the younger people. Following years of such frustration, several Indians sought for their guardian-spirit visions as they had done in their older faith and learned new power songs and dances. They reported that the spirits assured them that if the people sang and danced sufficiently, the recently deceased would come back to life, game would return, plant food would be available, and the hated whites would vanish, and all would be as it had been in the earlier golden times. The Indians organized themselves, built dance houses, and spread the ideology and its ceremonial accompaniments from village to village. After a while, the Ghost Dance cult weakened and fell into disuse.

The life-style of the Melanesian population of the South Seas is greatly varied. These people live in New Guinea, Vanuatu, Fiji, the Solomon Islands, and countless thousands of smaller islands throughout the vast South Pacific. It is certain, however, that the traumatic effect of the European arrival on the Melanesian populace in this area was severe. The trauma is exemplified by the bizarre cargo cults, which were, and in some cases still are, widespread throughout some of the islands. Most Melanesians generally believe that all material things are sent by spirits. Seeing that the Europeans had many riches, the Melanesians were, at first, eager to worship the same spirits as the Europeans. Early Christian missionaries met with great success; the newly converted expected to receive valuable treasures.

Many different cults have been identified and documented throughout the South Seas over many years, going back as far as 1885. The first on record was the Tuka Cult that occurred among the Fiji Islanders. In 1893, in Papua New Guinea, there was the Milne Bay Prophet Movement. The first cult that seemed to reflect cargo cult mentality began in 1913 on the island of Saibal in the Torres Straits of New Guinea. The cult followed the usual manifestations. The prophet would declare that the true believers would see their messiah (who was usually the spirit of a dead person). He would come in a large ship bringing all sorts of goods. Once there, he would drive out the white man.

Those in the village who disobeyed the leader would lose their pigs and their gardens would die. Misfortune would shadow their lives—their friends would ostracize them. The natives could only believe that the whites received all of their goods by ship from some unknown place. There seemed to be no evidence that the whites had anything to do with the making of anything, but "things" still belonged to them.

Another frustration of the native people was that they observed that the whites did little work, usually sitting at tables and writing on bits of paper. What sort of magic was this? Who made these materials that the whites obtained with such ease? How could it be for the white man, who appeared so lazy? The native people reasoned that the goods must be made in some unknown land by the spirits of their dead ancestors.

Over the years cults came and went; often they flared up for brief periods and then disappeared into the mists of time. The Baigona Snake Cult in Papua New Guinea between 1911 and 1920 was characterized by the people going into trances. This cult developed some nationalistic and political feelings.

One of the more fascinating of the cults was the Vailala Madness that occurred in New Guinea villages between 1919 and 1923. This cult was distinctive because of the practice of the people (urged on by their sorcerers) going into wild orgies of shaking, howling, shivering, and dreamlike dances. Strangely, Christian influences marked the cult. There was belief in the resurrection; deceased relatives would return wearing white skins; women were given equality with men—almost unheard of in New Guinea. But, like the other cults, its popularity faded with time.

Although most cults had strong elements of anti-white sentiment and occasionally displayed militancy, no acts of violence against the European settlers had taken place. This was to change. In 1923, the natives of Espiritu Santo, Vanuatu (formerly the New Hebrides), were excited by rumors of the dead returning to life. Their prophets announced that if all of the Europeans were killed, their own dead would arise from the graves, dressed in white skins. During a feast to honor this coming event, one of the prophet's wives died. The inflamed natives rushed to the home of a European living nearby, seized and killed him, and ate parts of his body.

The response by the British authorities to this act was swift and harsh. A gunboat was sent to shell the village and burn it to the ground. Marines were landed and three natives (supposedly ringleaders of the cult) were seized and taken to government headquarters. They were given a brief trial, found guilty, and hanged. After this, the cult was suppressed.

It became more apparent to the European authorities that the followers of the cargo cults on the islands that they occupied represented a distinct threat to their authority. Steps were taken to arrest the ringleaders, the messiahs, and the prophets. Arrests were made and jail sentences were meted out. Some of the more influential leaders were exiled to other islands.

There were a host of other cults, mostly led by native prophets. However, one cult, the Chair and Rule Movement, was led by a European missionary who actually encouraged the natives to seek an active voice in government. The strange name of this cult had a simple explanation. The people had observed the British administrator in his office, sitting at his desk and holding a ruler. Outside flew the British flag to emphasize his authority. Why not, reasoned the natives, do the same? So, they set up in their villages a table, chair, ruler, and flag pole, symbols of their own authority in their own village.

A harsher element in some of the cult movements was their self-destructiveness. The Markham Cargo Cult of Papua New Guinea (1932-34) prophesied earthquakes, floods, and destruction of the land. On the advice of their leaders, people destroyed their villages and trekked to the mountains. The leaders of the Buka cult on the island of Buka in the Solomons also prophesied that destructive earthquakes would destroy their land. After the earthquakes, however, a ship would arrive bringing food, clothing, and material goods. According to the prophets, as long as food was available in the gardens, the ship would not come.

Natives abandoned their gardens, uprooted their potato plants, and sat patiently in the village awaiting the arrival of the ship. Such behavior was completely unrewarding, often resulting in the starvation of entire villages, forcing the authorities to come to their rescue with rice and other foods. The fact that the cult was a failure was no assurance that it would lose its hold on the people. Failure might mean that the wrong ritual was used or that the prophets were false. There was always the possibility that the Europeans had a hand in the failure. The fact that the spirits did not arrive and did not bring the cargo did not mean that they did not exist.

Cargo cults continued to emerge and submerge throughout the South Pacific. Some failed because they were too self-destructive. Others were suppressed because of their open militancy against white authority. These cults were usually harshly suppressed by the police and their leaders and followers, if not arrested, would often go underground. When the Americans arrived in the South Pacific during World War II, some of the cults reemerged. The Americans quickly made a good reputation by their friendliness and their generosity. Black soldiers were seen working alongside whites and good paying jobs working for the army at the docks and around the camp were plentiful for the natives. To the natives, the Americans were something very special, unlike the repressive, authoritarian British colonists. Even today a residue of respect for the Americans remains with the people of the South Seas, as I have on so many occasions found.

One of the dominating features of cults is the desire of the followers either to return to the Golden Past* or to seek out the New Future. A cult is bound together by a system of religious worship. It is also a group bound together by devotion and reverence to a person or an ideal. To those who would choose to return to the Golden Past, it meant going back to the old "custom ways." To the natives of the South Seas, this meant giving up all vestiges of European culture: doing away with money, stopping attendance at Christian churches, discontinuing the wearing of European clothing, going back to the native dances and songs, drinking kava juice again, observing the village taboos and worship of the dead ancestors.

* The Ghost Dance cult of the American Indians of the West in 1870 was a good example of this.

*Chapter Ten*

# The John Frum Cult

Although traveling to other areas of the world, my main interest still lay in New Guinea. Attending school at UCLA in search of an advanced degree in anthropology, my interest now was becoming increasingly piqued by the rumors and stories of other cargo cults.

In the UCLA library one day I found a book entitled *John Frum, He Come*, by Edward Rice. Rice had visited the island of Tanna in Vanuatu to observe and study the cargo cult called the John Frum Cult that was still alive and active on the island when he first visited there in the early 1970s. It is still alive today, after having gone through tremendous changes from its original form in the late 1930s.

After reading the book, my interest was thoroughly aroused and nothing could keep me from making a visit to the island. Every Februry 15, on the island of Tanna, a festival is held to honor John Frum. I wanted to go to this event and study more of the fascinating story of John Frum. As usual, Stevey accompanied me. We departed for Vanuatu on February 7, 1977.

One of the most serious of the injustices that the white man perpetrated on the natives of the South Seas was the practice of "blackbirding." Boys and young men were recruited, sometimes forcibly, from their villages to go to work on large plantations, usually in Northern Australia. These men would be gone for years, some never to return. This practice not only depleted the village of many of its menfolk, but it also seriously altered the social structure and severely diminished whole islands of their population and left a legacy of bitterness toward the white man.

When missionaries moved into Tanna, they appropriated some of the best land for their own use, all in the name of God's work. The missionaries seriously believed that their work, in the name of God, would bring the true faith to the heathen natives and supersede everything else.

On Tanna, in 1940, there were signs of unrest among the natives. Half the male population had gone to work elsewhere because of the practice of "blackbirding." The fall in copra prices had badly hurt the economy and the missionaries and the government were pushing their reforms.

As if in answer to the people's frustrations, there suddenly appeared on the scene a prophet with the unusual name of John Frum.* He was described as a "mysterious little man with bleached hair, a high pitched voice and clad in a coat with shining buttons." In his excellent book *The Trumpet Shall Sound*, Peter Worseley describes in some detail what the arrival of John Frum must have been like and what effect it had on the people:

John Frum used ingenious stage management—appearing at night in dim light before men who were under the influence of kava. This prophet was regarded as the representative or earthly manifestation of Karaperamun, god

*Anthropologist Rentoni shares the name John Frum from "Broom" (Frum—the broom with which the whites could be swept from Tanna) and considers that "John" reflects the breakaway from John the Baptist Mission and the formation of an independent native church.

of the island's highest mountain. Karaperamun now appeared as John Frum, who was to be hidden from whites and women.

John Frum issued specific moral injunctions against idleness, encouraged communal gardening and cooperation, and advocated native dancing and kava drinking. He had no anti-white message at first. He also prophesied the occurrence of a cataclysm in which Tanna would become flat, mountains would fall and fill the river beds to form fertile plains, and Tanna would be joined with neighboring islands to form a new island. When this happened, John Frum would reveal himself, bringing a reign of bliss, the natives would get back their youth and there would be no sickness; there would be no need to care for gardens, trees or pigs. The Whites would go; John Frum would set up schools to replace mission schools and he would pay chiefs and school teachers.

There was only one difficulty. The presence and the power of the white man on Tanna had to be expelled. One method of eliminating the whites was to destroy their influence. A way to do this was to abandon all that the whites had brought with them or taught them. A first step was to give up European clothing. This was done with some reluctance, for shorts and shirts had a status symbol. Secondly, they must abandon the use of European money. While some of the people solved this problem by throwing it into the sea, others went on an orgy of spending at the trade stores. This created no serious problems because bartering between the natives had long been a way of life and every family had its own garden.

John Frum also preached the restoration of ancient "custom ways," many of which had been prohibited by both the government and the missionaries. The drinking of kava was revived—a practice frowned on by the missionaries for its narcotic effect. Native dances, thought too provocative by the church, were revived and polygamy was again practiced.

The killing of valuable pigs and feasting became more common. John Frum had prophesied that once the millennium had occurred there would be no further need to work the gardens. It would be provided for in light of the riches that were about to come.

In 1941, the British government became disturbed by the strength of the movement and its growing anti-white attitude and sought to suppress it. The man claiming to be John Frum was a native Tannese by the name of Mannehivi. He was arrested, tried, and sentenced to three years in jail and five years' exile.

Other prophets appeared on the scene, all claiming to be the "true" John Frum. One such prophet, Joe Nalpin, had a new theme. John Frum was King of America and Tanna. When the news reached Tanna that the Americans had actually arrived on Vila (staging for the Guadalcanal invasion in 1942), the followers of John Frum knew no bounds. All restraint was thrown to the wind and the people went into an orgy of drinking, dancing, and celebration.

When the war ended in 1945, the Americans left Vanuatu and life for the native people on Tanna gradually returned to its old colonial style. For a while high copra prices brought relative peace and prosperity. But the seeds of the John Frum cult remained and the movement began to take on a socio-religious form. Gradually, the need for such a movement diminished as the native people became more and more involved in trade, business, and commerce. The "true" believers in John Frum lessened but even those who didn't believe saw in the John Frum movement a rallying point for demanding social, economic, and political equality with the white man. One would not normally visit Vanuatu during February, for the weather is humid, hot, and rainy. But our visit was set by the date of the festival. Armed with tape recorder, motion picture equipment, and several thousand feet of film, we set out for Tanna, traveling by way of Tahiti, Noumea, and then on to Port Vila, capital of Vanuatu on the Island of Efate.

Vanuatu is an off-the-beaten-path experience. It was then a condominium, the only one in the world, ruled jointly by Great Britain and France. As a matter of fact, local wags referred to it as a "pandemonium." Vanuatu has a land mass of fifty-seven hundred square miles spread over seventy-three islands of varying sizes, stretching four hundred fifty miles in a north-south direction. Its terrain ranges from high mountains, heavy jungles, and smoking volcanoes to magnificent coral reefs and golden beaches.

After several days outfitting in Vila, we set out for Tanna on February 9. Air Melanesia had twice daily flights to Tanna by a twin-engined, ten-passenger plane whose schedule is totally dependent upon the tricky weather and the grass landing strip, which is sometimes flooded.

Our flight to Tanna could best be described as "hairy." We flew south 140 miles in the middle of a blinding rainstorm and the last twenty minutes were spent at six hundred feet looking for the island. There was no radio communication to give the pilot instructions.

We finally landed on a beautiful, rolling grass strip and were met by our host, Bob Paul. Bob, a long-time Australian resident of Tanna, owned the local trade store as well as the only available accommodations on the island. A simple, self-contained bungalow could be rented for eleven dollars a night. We bought food from Bob's trade store or at the local native market in Lanakel, a few miles away from our bungalow.

The origins of John Frum are many and varied and depend upon whom you might be speaking to on Tanna or what anthropological research book or journal you might have been reading. One favorite version was that he was an American medical corpsman who promised the natives shiploads of presents and preached to them a smattering of socialism and independence. But the story repeated to me most often was that John Frum first made his appearance at Ipekel on Tanna about 1940. Reports began to circulate among the natives that a supernatural being was promising a millennium with all the material goods the people desired. John Frum predicted that there would be a big war; he would bring the Americans to Vanuatu and they would have fabulous amounts of cargo they would share with the people.

But the conditions set down by John Frum to bring all of this to pass required that the people break away from European customs and return to their old ways and customs. Kava drinking (a mild intoxicant made from the root of the kava bush) was severely criticized by the missionaries. Now it was once again to become a daily custom. Traditional dancing was resumed and the mission churches were virtually deserted. European money was spent quickly because it was rumored it would soon become useless.

When the Americans did arrive in Vanuatu, which was the staging point for the invasion of the Solomon Islands, great numbers of Tannese went to Port Vila to receive employment, loading or unloading ships or building roads and warehouses. The natives observed black troops living and working on an equal basis with white soldiers. The Americans were generous, paid well, and treated the natives with open friendliness—something few Europeans did.

The symbol of the John Frum Cult on Tanna is a wooden cross, painted red. It is found in many locations on Tanna and is reverently worshiped by the believers. Legend has it that Nambas, a young Tannese working for the American army in Vila during the war, acquired a jacket from a Red Cross worker. This young man already had become a believer in John Frum and he told his friends, "I have seen John Frum; he promises he will come; he will bring cargo; the Red Cross is his symbol; you must worship and respect it." Until his death, Nambas was the leader of the John Frum Society at Sulphur Bay in Tanna.

When the war ended, it was followed by a period of disappointment for the people of Vanuatu. The Americans disappeared. The cargo ships no longer came. There were few jobs and the Europeans resumed their old, colonial style of living, dominating the natives and suppressing their desire for independence.

John Frum's promises had failed to materialize and there were new repressions on the part of the Anglo-French government against cult members. Leaders were often jailed or exiled, and some of the Tannese began drifting back to the mission churches and schools. But the cult was far from dead, as we soon found out on our arrival at Tanna.

Part of the legend of John Frum is built around the active volcano of Yasur near Sulphur Bay. Yasur is still very much alive and we reached it by land over a very rough eighteen-mile road from Lanakel. The final approach was across a lunar-like volcanic ash bed. The stench of sulphur fumes was overpowering and about every twenty seconds Yasur let out a low-throated roar.

We climbed to its nine-hundred-foot high rim after a fairly strenuous thirty-minute hike in ankle-deep ash. Our reward was a spectacular flop because it had rained so heavily the day before that we were greeted by one vast blanket of steam and smoke. Peering down over the rim we could make out nothing, but could hear the volcano grumbling, hissing, and bubbling: Just as we turned to leave, Yasur exploded, sending rocks high into the air and reminding us that we were treading on sacred ground.

Yasur is sacred to the John Frum people and you must engage an escort from Sulphur Bay to climb it. Under no circumstances must you touch or remove any of the rocks on the slope, for they, too, are sacred.

Some of the cult members believe that John Frum has an army of from five thousand to twenty thousand soldiers in the volcano waiting to come out at the messiah's bidding and drive the white man from Tanna. This disparity in numbers usually depends on how much kava the storyteller has been drinking or how devout are his beliefs.

Our nights at our bungalow were usually lonely and always rainy; few other guests seemed to be about. For meals, Stevey would often heat up a can of meat, slice and fry some yams or taro, and we would wash it down with hot coffee, tea, or an occasional bottle of wine. We were adopted by a family of cats whose gesture of friendship was to drop their dead rats on our floor every morning.

During the nine days spent on Tanna we saw the sun but twice. The rest of the time was a contest with the flies, mosquitoes and other buzz bombing insects, and the unremitting rain. It was here, at Lanakel, that I contracted a bad dose of malaria.

Since a return to "custom ways" was part of the acceptance of the John Frum cults, a word here should be said about the drinking of kava. Kava is made from the root of the kava bush (*Piper Methysticum*). Its consumption each evening by the men of the village can only be likened to that of the Australian stopping off at his favorite pub each evening to quaff his drink. My own experience with kava leads me to speak on the subject as a poor expert.

One day Tom asked us if we would like to go to a barbecue. I had visions of smoked hams, roast suckling pig, and quantities of beer. Actually, the barbecue turned out to be a political rally for one of the local native independence parties. It was a rather quiet and subdued affair, with all the men and women standing in separate groups under umbrellas. It was pouring rain, as usual.

I made a special request to visit the men's hut where the kava drinking was taking place and to partake in this little ceremony. But my stomach was not quite prepared for what followed. While the older, married men squatted on their haunches and chatted, the unmarried boys and men prepared the root.

The kava root (usually about one inch thick) was cleaned by scrubbing with a coconut husk. Then it was the turn of the married men to begin chewing the roots, masticating them into a pulp and spitting the pulp into a wooden bowl where it was mixed with water and allowed to ferment.

The unmarried men then commenced kneading the masticated kava until it was ready to be mixed with more water. Then they strained it through a porous leaf into half a coconut shell. The kava was now ready to drink.

Being a guest, I was offered the first bowl. Forewarned that it was a custom to drink the whole bowl in one draft, I tried, but failed. Halfway through the first swallow, my stomach warned me to go slowly. Who knows what the penalty might be for throwing up a bowl of kava? I was in no condition to find out. At a nearby hut, another drinking party was in progress where beer and whisky were served.

It is also the custom that women are absolutely forbidden to drink kava, or even so much as watch the men prepare and drink it. If a woman does make the mistake of observing the event, she is beaten, usually with a kava bush. Our party was inside a hut, so it would have been difficult for any outsider to observe our doings. Nevertheless, when three women passed nearby, the men threatened and warned them away.

One bowl of kava was all I could manage and its only effect was a slight numbness around the mouth. Bob Gregory, a local American anthropologist, told me that he had consumed as many as twelve bowls at one get-together and had become quite stoned and unable to stand up or walk steadily. He reported that the kava also made the eyes quite sensitive to light and produced a decided irritation to noise. As a consequence, most kava parties were silent, contemplative affairs.

One of the extraordinary features of the John Frum cult is its followers' belief in their power to transmit messages by imitation radios and telephones. Tom, a native Tannese and our driver on numerous occasions, told me of his unusual experience with a "flower radio." Tom viewed most John Frum activities somewhat skeptically, so I felt that he was not exaggerating the incident.

Tom said that one day he was in a small, isolated village in the north of Tanna talking to a friend. He told his friend of a trip he was about to make to Vila the following day. (Vila is on the island of Efate, 140 air miles to the north.) His friend said he would have his son meet

Tom at the airport at Vila on arrival. Tom knew this was impossible because the only wireless station was on Tanna, many miles distant, and there would be no way nor time to transmit a message from Tanna to Vila for at least several days and Tom told his friend so. Tom's friend was insistent and said, "Excuse me, I shall go inside my home and talk to my flower radio." This he did, explaining to Tom that his son had a similar flower in his pocket in Vila. Vibrations of the flower told him when a message was being sent by his father. The next day when Tom arrived in Vila by plane, his friend's son was waiting there to meet him! To many this would be an extraordinary example of ESP.

Our first week on Tanna, awaiting the event of the John Frum celebration at Sulphur Bay, passed quickly enough, although the constant rain and cloud cover were depressing. One day I took a walk to visit the village of Iakukek, for I had learned through Bob Paul that Bob Gregory was living there with his wife, doing research It was a long, muddy hike up a jungle trail that had once been a road, but the rain had made it into a stream. Very few people were about, but there were many pigs rummaging in the bush. At one point I thought I was lost and when I spotted two children I shouted in pidgin, "Where haus belong Bob?" The children fled in panic. But I followed their path and came to a tiny village where a man offered me directions to Tuk's house.

I had met Tuk before in Lanakel. His English was reasonably good and we could usually engage in understandable conversations. Tuk was one of the important leaders of the John Frum cult on Tanna and being the chief of Iakukek, his word carried considerable authority. During our numerous conversations, Tuk had repeatedly emphasized to me that the John Frum cult members at

Sulphur Bay (where the festival was to be held) were not "true" or "custom" cult members.

Tuk explained to me that the true John Frum followers were from the Lanakel area of Tanna, which coincidentally, also happened to be his area. Tuk considered that the marching drills conducted by the people at Sulphur Bay during the festival were not true to John Frum because they represented a militaristic attitude that could not be considered characteristic of the Tannese people, who are not warlike or, at least, don't want their problems with the Europeans solved in a military way.

The people at Sulphur Bay contend that their marching and drilling military formations was not an act of preparing themselves for war against the Europeans, but a sign of social unity. In fact, the pre-European history of Tanna indicates that it was an extremely warlike society with much evidence of tribal wars and in the early days cannibalism and headhunting were common practices.

I asked Tuk where he thought John Frum was now and he answered, "I don't know, maybe in America, maybe in the spirit world; but he will return and on his return he will help the Tannese people obtain independence, more cargo, and greater happiness." At least in one sense, he was right, for the people are now independent.

Not even the Tannese agree as to the color of John Frum's skin. Some say he is a white man, possibly an American. Tom Hiwa, a respected John Frum leader from Lanakel, told me that John Frum has seven different skins, all black and all young, which he often changes so that he can pass unnoticed among his people!

Tuk's village of Iakukek was completely unlike the "Christianized" mission villages along the coast and near

the government stations. The mission villages tended to
be laid out as compounds, the homes usually surrounding
a community recreational field or church. This was a by-
product of the early missionaries who tried to bring the
flock close to the church or mission station.

## *Chapter Eleven*

# Sulphur Bay

We were awakened at 6:00 A.M. on the morning of February 15, 1977 by Tom, who was to drive us to Sulphur Bay to witness the John Frum festival. Our fellow passengers were Tuk and a young Australian couple. The road was rough, little better than a jeep trail. The rain had reduced it to quagmire conditions.

Crowds of people were traveling the road on foot, all on their way to the festival—men, women, children, and even small babies being carried in their mothers' arms. Everyone was dressed in their best and it was a colorful sight despite the dampening rain. Some of the natives must have started four or five hours earlier because we recognized people from Lanakel, eighteen miles behind us.

The village of Sulphur Bay was built in the Christian mission fashion, the homes formed in a square surrounding a large, flat, grass-covered field, roughly the size of two footfall fields. In the center of the village square was a single red-painted cross surrounded by a low fence—John Frum's symbol. Several huge banyan trees offered cover for spectators.

A large gaily dressed crowd had already gathered and they stood rather quietly watching the arrival of others, suffering the rain under their large, black umbrellas. Incoming "traffic" was being directed by the most incongruous-looking native of very stern demeanor who was barefoot, in a T-shirt and shorts, armed with a billy club, and wearing an American army helmet. There was to be no funny business here.

The "traffic" actually consisted of about a dozen Land Rovers—some owned by local French and British, or more affluent Tannese. Some of the vehicles were working as sort of a shuttle taxi service, bringing people from the more distant villages. This was an important occasion on Tanna—a once-a-year happening that attracted believers and nonbelievers from every part of Tanna and some of the offshore islands.

While we stood waiting for the activities to start, Tuk wasted no opportunity to reiterate to me that the Sulphur Bay people were not the "number one" John Frum cultists, because the John Frum cult had originally started at Lanakel. He offered to explain that the people at Sulphur Bay were once called the Isaac cult (Isaac was rumored to have been one of John Frum's sons) but, for reasons unexplained, they decided to borrow the John Frum name and make it their own.

Suddenly a hush fell over the crowd at Sulphur Bay and all eyes were centered on the cross in the center of the village. A small group of Tannese men and women, all dressed in European clothes, approached the cross and stopped. In their hands they held flowers. Their arms were supplicantly held across their chests.

Then, quietly and softly, the group began to sing hymnlike music that was not unlike what we had heard in the Presbyterian church the Sunday before. It was a song of praise to John Frum sung in pidgin. The singing completed, the group knelt before the cross, extending their hands, still holding the flowers toward John Frum's symbol. Finally, individuals moved forward and placed their flowers upon the cross, completing this act of worship and faith to their absent messiah.

I found the experience deeply moving but could not help but be impressed with the involvement the John Frum cult seemed to have with aspects of the Christian church. If they have rejected the church's ideals, they have not rejected many of its ways. The work of early missionaries had left its mark.

I had to set up my movie camera on the edge of the crowd. It was still raining. Stevey assisted me by holding an umbrella over my head. A new phase of the ceremony was commencing and our attention was turned to the far end of the field.

There appeared a company of about fifty men, marching two abreast and advancing into the center of the village square. The only sound, except for the sharp orders of the drill sergeant, was the pounding of their feet, made more pronounced by the resonance of the volcanic bed beneath them.

I had been told what to expect, but I was not prepared for this spectacle. It was as impressive, in its own way, as the changing of the guard at Buckingham Palace. The men were shirtless and shoeless, some wearing long trousers, others in shorts. Each marching man carried a rifle made of bamboo over his shoulder which was topped with an imitation bayonet painted red. On his chest and sometimes on his back were painted in red the letters U.S.A.!

The men marched with precision and in the British army's military style, high knee action and swinging arms. The orders were barked in English. The marchers were stern-faced. The mood of the crowd was solemn.

For the next hour different drill teams made their appearance, each group representing men from other John Frum villages in and around Sulphur Bay or some of the offshore islands. All age groups seemed to be represented, from young boys to mature men.

How does one explain the meaning behind this impressive and touching ceremony? The answers are many and varied. Probably no single explanation offers the correct answer. Many stories link the John Frum cult with America. One legend relates that John Frum was an American Seabee who arrived with the American troops during World World II. This Seabee was said to have preached a smattering of socialism and equality to the hired native dock workers. The generous American soldier struck a note of sympathy with the people and left them with feelings of respect and admiration. The American had not come to exploit them; his ships and planes had brought the promised cargo. John Frum, whomever he was, preached to his people that one day they would share in Americans' wealth. The years of exploitation would be gone forever and the people of Tanna would be the masters of their own fate.

The rest of the day was devoted to a series of dance exhibitions performed by men, women, and children. Most of these dances depicted hunting, fishing, food gathering, and one particularly amusing performance was a pantomime boxing match.

A recess from the dancing was taken for the people to eat and feast. The main food was *lap lap*, a cooked mixture of taro, sweet potatoes, yams, and coconut milk. Occasionally, meat was added to this. The *lap lap*, which was wrapped in banana leaves, was contributed mainly by visitors from other villages, who stacked it in a large pile in the village center—but the *lap lap* was stacked in such a manner that those who had prepared a particular *lap lap* would never make the mistake of taking and eating their own, which would have been considered in very bad taste.

After the ceremony was over and we had returned

to Lanakel, I couldn't help but ask Tuk if he was disappointed and disillusioned by the failure of John Frum to return with the promised cargo. He replied, "You Christians have waited two thousand years for Jesus Christ to return; we can wait a few years for John Frum."

*Chapter Twelve*

# The Solomon Islands

During my studies and inquiries about cargo cults of the South Seas I learned of another famous one, the Maasina cult, located in the Are Are Lagoon of South Malaita, Solomon Islands. In May of 1978 we were again headed for the South Seas.

A revolutionary, antiwhite cult—the Maasina Rule Movement—appeared first in the Solomon Islands in 1945. It was sometimes called the Marching Rule cult, the Moro Customs Company and, by the British colonists, the Marxist cult.*

The Maasina cult (as I shall refer to it hereafter) was the most politically oriented of all of the cults that had yet appeared and had its birth on the island of Malaita, undoubtedly partly a by-product of the war.

Heavy fighting took place between the Japanese and American troops on Guadacanal in 1942. Although the war disrupted the natives' lives, the presence of the Americans had an even greater effect. They came with an armada of ships, tanks, airplanes, and guns. They were generous to the natives and offered ample job opportunities. When the fighting ended and the Americans

* There is no evidence that the Maasina cult had any Marxist influence.

moved on, the old order returned with the British administration reestablishing its former colonial style government. A strong anti-British sentiment began to manifest
itself among the native people.

The leader of the Maasina cult was a man named
Nori.* While on a fishing trip, Nori was taken ill and
became unconscious. His friends thought he was dead and
made arrangements for his funeral. But Nori recovered
and told his friends of the "vision" he had experienced
while unconscious. He told them a man in the vision told
him, "Everything in this land, the mountains, the seas,
the trees, the gardens, belongs to you and your people.
You must start a company to make money. All the things
that are yours should be used."

Nori and his vision were incorporated into a charter
for a socio-religious movement, which aimed at establishing a political organization at its head. Attempts were
made to establish native-owned cooperative business ventures. Demonstrations took place against the British, and
missionary and administrative work was resisted. Higher
wages for work done for the Europeans were demanded,
as well as better education and political independence.
The movement spread from Malaita to Guadalcanal and
the Santa Cruz islands. The British recognized the
strength of this new cult and realized that gunboat diplomacy was no longer effective. Here was the first determined effort by the government to boost the economy of
the islands. Agriculturists were sent to native villages to
help increase copra production and to plant better-yielding garden produce.

Despite this, it was not enough to stop the spread of
the Maasina cult. Nori and his followers continued to

*A Solomon Island patriot and politician, Mr. Johathan Fifi, contributed most of this information on the Maasina rule.

gain new recruits and collect large sums of money and the people continued to resist working for the Europeans or attending the missionary schools.

Although the basic tenets of the cult were independence from the British rule and a desire for economic independence, it still retained some of the mysticism of the older cults as well. Warehouses were built to store the goods that the Americans would bring on their return. Unlike other cults, however, the Maasina movement did not seek to return to the Golden Past. Nori and his followers believed that they must change their way of living to adapt to a modern world that was rapidly encroaching on them. All they asked was that they be allowed to fashion their own way without interference from the white man.

The Are Are Lagoon is a remote area, not visited by tourists and reachable only by boat. It was necessary for me to obtain special permission from the government who, in turn, would have to receive the approval of the village chief, for we would be his guest. Armed with more hope than confidence, Stevey and I set out on our journey.

The soldiers who fought on these remote islands during the war years of 1942–45 experienced humid heat, tropical ulcers, deadly malaria, near starvation, exhaustion, and death. When told of our intention to visit the Solomons, an ex-marine said, "Man, you must be crazy!"

The war ended more than three decades ago, and today the islands enjoy peace and quiet and an undisturbed remoteness. Discovered by the Spanish sailor/ explorer Alvero de Mendana in 1567, they were named for the biblical King Solomon's mines in the hope that evidence of gold discovered in the jungle-clad mountains of one of the islands might lead to much more. The gold did not materialize and the islands were forgotten by European explorers for the next two hundred years. The Melanesians who inhabited the islands continued their savage ways of cannibalism, headhunting, and tribal wars.

The British established a protectorate over the Solomon Islands in 1893 and ruled the islands until recently. The Solomon Islands celebrated their first year of independence on July 17, 1979. Most of the islands consider themselves more or less independent of each other. A serious attempt, however, is made to work harmoniously as a country and appears to be quite successful, although the people share only pidgin as a common language.

Time, distance, and transportation are the primary concerns for the traveler in the South Seas. It is usually possible to travel anywhere, but patience is the key. Usually nothing runs on time, distances are vast (Los Angeles to Honiara, the capital, is about ten thousand miles), and modes of transportation can be a combination of aircraft, truck, canoe, and foot.

Honiara, on the north coast of Guadalcanal, does not have an attractive climate. It has a worn, jaded air. Everyone wilts in the fierce midday heat.

On the advice of friends, we booked into the Hibiscus Hotel, also known as "Hepatitis House" and by other less complimentary names. This was our good fortune for, while not noted for its kitchen, its bedrooms, or other amenities, it is the best place to stay if you are interested in meeting the important and interesting local people.

It was while staying at the Hibiscus that we met and became good friends with David Kusimae, once member of parliament from Malaita; John Gina, prominent citizen and holder of the Order of the British Empire (O.B.E.); his brother Lloyd, who was Speaker of the House, as well as many others whose knowledge and involvement in the affairs of these islands made our visit more enjoyable and rewarding. They all seemed to gather for morning coffee and afternoon tea at the Hibiscus Hotel.

I really hadn't intended staying in Honiara any longer than necessary, except to collect my government permits to visit, film, and document the people and cultural life of villages on other more remote islands. Getting my permits out of the Ministry of cultural Affairs was a bit like pulling teeth. While waiting, I visited the battlefields of World War II that gave Guadalcanal its infamous reputation.

Anyone even vaguely acquainted with the war in the South Pacific will remember such grimly nostalgic names as Red Beach, Henderson Field, Bloody Ridge, Cape Esperance, Iron Bottom Sound, and the Toyoko Express as bloody reminders of the battle of Guadalcanal in 1942. One afternoon we rented a car and drove out to Red Beach, site of the first American landing on Guadalcanal. Today, it is a quiet deserted strip of glistening white sand edging a coconut plantation. The quiet, lapping surf and white sands hide memories of a grim past. Hunks of rusting metal, scattered here and there on the sand and in the water, mark the remains of landing boats abandoned by the Americans after the invasion.

On the way back to Honiara, and after a prolonged search, we located the village of California, renamed by its local chief, Joseph Vouza, in honor of the American Marine Corps. Vouza is a Solomon Island legend. While acting as a scout for the marines in 1942, Vouza was captured by the Japanese, tied to a tree and tortured, bayoneted, and left for dead. Vouza managed to escape and crawl back to the marine lines with important information before collapsing. For this the Marine Corps made Vouza an honorary sergeant major, decorated him with the Silver Star, and sent him on a trip to the United States. We had a good visit, swapped war stories and, while I took many pictures, Vouza reminded me that "Things haven't been much good on Guadalcanal since the marines went home."

After a week, despairing of any immediate action out of the Ministry of Cultural Affairs, we decided to explore the Western Province of the Solomon Islands by booking passage on the *Independence*, a three-hundred-ton cargo passenger ship that made a once-a-week trip to the islands in the west.

To call the *Independence* a passenger ship is generous. She carried about 250 passengers (with room for fifty), two toilets, no galley (for which we probably could be thankful) and a crew that seemed forever asleep in some corner of the ship. We booked "bridge lounge," which turned out to be a rather small, top-deck cabin outfitted with ten reclining chairs for sleeping and, as we later discovered, a resident rat or two. The fare to Gizo for the two-day, overnight trip was cheap.

Although it was a bring-your-own-food arrangement, we quickly learned that at the many frequent island harbor stops along the way, the local people sold ample supplies of fresh *paw paw*, pineapples, breadfruit, taro, sweet potatoes, tapioca pudding (native style, wrapped in leaves), and generous amounts of bananas and coconuts. Betel nut, the famous nut that the natives chew for its mild narcotic effect, was also available.

But for all her faults, the ancient, battered *Independence* was a happy ship, a beehive of activity, and a mixture of many friendly people. The few Europeans on the boat and the islanders mixed freely and congenially. Most Solomon Islanders speak some English or, if not, usually know pidgin. The quaint language is laced with many half-English, half-native words that can usually be understood after a few days' exposure and trial. If you don't like someone, try telling him in pidgin he's "one fella something nothing." He will get the point.

Most of the traveling islanders were on their way home after a visit to the "big city" of Honiara to shop, visit relatives, or go to one of the outer islands on business. There was a scattering of Europeans on board, an American anthropologist and his wife, several vacationing Australians, and an Englishman returning home with his native wife.

Traveling westward, the ship *Independence* touched briefly at the Russells, a group of idyllic, coral-fringed islands dominated by coconut trees swaying gracefully in the offshore breezes. On our starboard side loomed the tall, brooding mountains of New Georgia, which, covered in whirling mist, dropped abruptly down to the sea. On the port side, sometimes only an arm's length away, the mangrove-covered islands kept our skipper ever alert, threading through the narrow passage.

After a while, the names of the harbor stops and islands became meaningless—Naggatokae, Yanguma, Mbatuna, Rendova, to name but a few. Each stop harbored a new experience, a new delight. There were several tiny unknown villages, unspoiled by roads, cars, or electricity. Their inhabitants' main concern in life was to get the gardens planted, cut down the coconuts, fish the lagoon and, perhaps once a week, check down at the dock to see who might be coming in on the *Independence*.

Just west of New Georgia, Kolombangara Island lifted its lofty fifty-eight-hundred-foot volcanic peak into a dense mass of ever-present clouds. It was between here and nearby Gizo Island in 1943 that a Japanese destroyer sliced through John F. Kennedy's PT Boat 109. It was off Kolombangara to Plum Pudding Island in Blackett Straits that Kennedy and the survivors of this mishap swam to await rescue. As we chugged past the island, many of the passengers pointed out "Kennedy's" island to us.

The Vanavoua Lagoon along New Georgia's northwest coast was a tropical paradise. The boat's passage was so narrow at times that one could almost touch the palm trees lining the bank. At moments the lagoon blazed under a fierce sun; minutes later it was drenched in pouring rain. Most of the passengers ignored the weather, sometimes stripping down for a bath when it rained! All along the way, frequent stops at small, native harbors were the occasion for noisy family reunions and brisk but brief trade at the village markets.

It was on this trip that I made my observation of the Solomon Islanders' personality; no one ever seemed to ask for help, but it was always freely offered; no tips were passed; no angry shouts or cries were heard. Everything was accomplished with relaxed, pleasant ease. Time was on the side of these people and they knew it.

We disembarked at the Island of Gizo, one of the westernmost of the Solomon Islands. Gizo has a neglected harbor of no special interest and one definitely third-rate hotel, where we were obliged to stay. The manager of the hotel got very drunk that night and sang his praise of the Americans (whom he apparently liked very much) in front of our door until he was carried off by friends. The only reason for our stopover at Gizo was to pay a visit to the local bank, the only place in the Western Solomons where travelers' checks could be cashed.

We completed our visit to the Western Solomons with a flight up to Kieta Bougainville, now part of Papua New Guinea. Kieta, I regret to say, is a sorry example of what mining money, modernization, and civilization can do to a primitive native culture. Thatched native huts have given way to prefabricated housing. Once quiet harbors are now dominated by giant ore tankers and their accompanying noise and dust. Most village gardens are gone, replaced by supermarkets with superprices. Perhaps worst of all was the amount of drunkenness among these good people—a sorry tribute to a primitive culture being destroyed by too much money too fast.

A lasting memory of Bougainville, however, was an incident at the airport customs house. Here, the barefooted customs agent passed my expensive movie camera, tape recorder, and film without question, only to reserve special attention to my straw hat, a simple thing bought in Honolulu almost as an afterthought. The hatband, made of dyed chicken feathers, must have represented to the customs agent a threat to the health of the state of the country and had to be confiscated. I watched in silence as he removed the hatband and plucked off the chicken feathers, which he then allowed to float away in the morning breeze.

From Gizo, we returned by plane southeastward to Munda, a small town on the island of New Georgia. The twin-engined, nine-passenger Beechcraft had no copilot, but the bush pilot knew his business and the flight over the coral-studded reefs, palm covered islands, and jungle topped mountains was filled with visual excitement.

Anyone visiting Munda must stay at Agnes Lodge, the village's one and only hotel. Quiet, unpretentious, and simple, with food and lodging to match, the secret of the charming, tiny, waterfront hotel, tucked away beneath palm trees, was Agnes, the part-English, part-Melanesian proprietress. Agnes was everyone's relative in town (quite literally) and everyone's friend. She presided over a host of duties—as general manager, cook, family arbitrator, and village counselor.

Plump, busy, and joyful, Agnes made the stranger feel immediately at home. I will hold lasting memories of evenings on the lodge veranda, with a pleasantly cool breeze blowing, engaged in animated conversation with Agnes and her small host of guests. Across the bay, the beautifully cylindrical volcanic cone of Rendova Island loomed up from the ocean like a sentinel on duty watching over the surrounding islands.

After more than three weeks of travel about the Solomon Islands, we returned to Honiara to see if our government permits had been issued. The island of Malaita is an area where strangers are not particularly welcome unless they have a valid reason and official permission for their visit.

The Malaitans are not unfriendly to strangers but most of the island is still primitive and undeveloped, and visitors would have nowhere to stay unless they were the guest of a village and have nothing to eat but what might be found in native gardens.

By reputation, the Malaitans are the most aggressive of all the Solomon Islanders. This may be partly due to the terrain of the island, which for the most part is rugged and mountainous and covered with heavy jungle. This has made for a shortage of tillable land on this overpopulated island. The Malaitans throughout their history have been extremely aggressive and feared, raiding other islands frequently for food, women, and other spoils they may have found hard to come by on Malaita.

*Chapter Thirteen*

# The Are Are Lagoon

Once again we were faced with a problem—how to get there. Our goal was southern Malaita. This is not an area frequented by tourists and it took some planning.

Auki, on the northwestern tip of Malaita, is the main port of entry and is serviced daily by a flight from Honiara or a once-a-week boat. When we learned that traveling by boat was a rough, time-consuming voyage, we turned our trust once again to the bush pilot. That was fine until we were airborne over Florida Island and our pilot decided to "buzz" some of his friends enjoying a Sunday picnic on a small tropical island below. Many of his passes were far too close for comfort.

We stayed in Auki just long enough to pick up additional permits and maps and arrange our transport to the south, as well as mend our ulcerating bites and infections at the local hospital. While waiting for the medic to treat me, I noticed a sign on the hospital door that put Medicare, Blue Cross, and all the others in their proper place. The sign read: "Important Notice: As from Monday, 4 March, all people who come to the outpatients will have to bring more potatoes if they come outside of normal hours. The new charges will be, Monday–Friday, 7:00 A.M. to 4:00 P.M. charge one potato; Monday–Friday, 4:00 P.M. to 6:00 P.M. charge five potatoes; Monday–Friday 6:00 P.M. to 7:00

P.M. charge ten potatoes. Everyone must bring potatoes. Only genuine emergencies will be seen without potatoes."

In a conversation with David Ruthvin, then permanent secretary of the Malaita council, it was decided that our most profitable visit would be with the people living in the Are Are* Lagoon area. In order to do this, we had to travel down the west coast by canoe and spend a week as the guests of the village of Wairokai. Arrangements for the trip would be made by advising the village chief of our government permits, time of arrival, and, most important, of our interest in studying and filming native "custom ways" of life. Since someone in the village was always sure to have a radio, word of our arrival could be sent over the evening newscast. No roads to Wairokai exist; there is no telephone line and boats only occasionally stop at the village.

We traveled light. We had two pairs of shorts apiece, two shirts, hats, sandals, and a teapot. What the village would be willing or able to provide us with was uncertain, until we talked with Todd McClintock, a former Peace Corps volunteer working for the Solomon Islands government in Auki. By good luck, Todd had been to Wairokai and knew the village and its people. He lent us two cots and a gas lantern that were to prove invaluable to us at Wairokai.

Our small party left Auki harbor early Tuesday morning of May 28, 1978. There were three of us, Chuck Wilkinson, Stevey, and myself. With us were two canoe operators and a government official to smooth our entrance to the village. The canoes were twenty-one–foot fiberglass boats equipped with outboard engines. Into these, we loaded our cots, lamps, duffle bags, enough food to last for a week, and our filming and sound equipment.

* Pronounced Arey Arey.

The voyage by canoe down Malaita's east coast took four hours, partly on open seas, partly through lagoons. Out on the open sea, it was a backbreaking experience as the canoe slapped and bounced its way over the heavy ocean swells, pounding mercilessly. Sometimes we traveled dangerously close to the coral reefs. I dwelled uncomfortably on the thought of an engine failure.

On entering the Langa Langa Lagoon, I was surprised by the sight of many "artificial" islands. Over the years the local people had constructed from coral, rock, and mud numerous islands in the lagoon built on shoal passages that rose just above the shallow water. Here families tended their coconut trees.

We entered the Are Are Lagoon at noon and cruised south for an hour, enjoying the peace and serenity of its smooth waters and unspoiled charm. Tiny villages along the coast appeared peaceful in the broiling midday sun. The offshore islands, mostly uninhabited because of their swampy conditions, were covered with mangrove trees and other shrubs. A few higher islands were heavily planted with coconut trees, the prized possession of some mainlanders. Once in a while, we saw fishermen out in their canoes trolling for fish in the lagoon.

Our arrival at Wairokai in midafternoon went virtually unnoticed, for the children were away at school and the adults were out working in their gardens. Only the oldsters were at home, tending the babies and the cooking fires.

Toward evening, the people began drifting home from their gardens. We were soon greeted by our official host, sub-chief Japhlet Kousana, who was also the village schoolteacher. Japhlet, who spoke good English, immediately put us at ease and guided us to the guest house where we would make our home for a week.

The guest house was built entirely of native thatching

material and its floor was raised about three feet off the ground to avoid flooding during heavy rains. Our room was plain, simple, and unfurnished. We were grateful for the loan of the two cots by our friend in Auki. Otherwise, we would have slept on the floor, as did most of the villagers.

Soon we met Benny, our landlord and cook. Skinny, dour, and taciturn, Benny lived in another barely furnished room with his wife, affectionately known as Mrs. Ben, and their small children. Mrs. Ben was short, stocky, jet black, and completely bald. She went about bare-breasted, usually carrying her infant son under one arm. A third room in the hut was reserved for the other visitors.

Although not accustomed to strangers, the villagers treated us with warmth and consideration. They spoke to us readily, if they spoke English. They usually waited until they were addressed, a custom we noticed throughout the Solomons and perhaps attributable to a natural shyness toward alien visitors.

Within a week we became accustomed to the life of the village. Since we neither worked in the gardens nor spoke the local language, our exposure was brief and cursory. Nevertheless, it was in sharp contrast to our life as city dwellers. In its simplicity it offered us an unusual but pleasant experience.

One of our first adjustments to village life was to acquaint ourselves with the toilet system. There were no groundholes, outhouses, or the like in the village. The toilet was "out in the ocean," men in one designated area, women in another. Our ingrained American modesty often found this embarrassing and sometimes downright uncomfortable. We soon learned to frequent a nearby river where the circumstances were far more comfortable and considerably less public.

Wairokai did have a piped water system with water supplied from a tank on a nearby hill and gravity fed to the village below. Outdoor showers and faucets were spaced throughout the village at convenient locations. Since the climate was always hot and muggy, frequent showers were most welcome. Swimming in the ocean was not popular, because of the danger of sharks.

The village had no electricity. All lighting was by wood fires, gas lanterns, or candlelight. We blessed Todd, once again, for the timely loan of his lantern, for which we had frequent use. Cooking was done over wood fires on the dirt floors of the cooking hut, which was located just next to the family home. These fires were kept going constantly.

To travel anywhere, except by foot to one's garden, a canoe is absolutely essential to these Malaitans. No roads exist in this area, perhaps never will, because of the rugged and mountainous terrain surrounding Wairokai. Once there were "bush people" living in the jungle nearby, but most have now moved to the coast for the safety and comfort of village life.

In Wairokai, as in most villages on Malaita, the people depend upon their gardens for staples and buy little other food from the outside. They grow a wide variety of fruits and vegetables: taro, sweet potatoes, peppers, bananas, breadfruit, paw paw, and pineapples. The staple food is the potato and is usually eaten two or three times a day. Benny regularly served us taro cooked in coconut milk for dinner, often mixed with either cabbage or fish, which we found delicious. When visiting other villages in the area during the day, we were often offered freshly roasted potatoes hot off the glowing coals of a wood fire.

Coconut meat was the village's main and only export.

Husked, dried, and sacked, the copra was shipped out by the weekly boat to Honiara. This export provided a small cash income for the village. Samuel Kasouna, Wairokai's chief, was growing peppers in his garden as a possible crop for curry makers in Quadalcanal.

Most village markets, even on Guadalcanal, were rather poorly stocked and uninteresting, a curious contrast to other native markets around the world. However, few people needed to buy anything; their own gardens provided most of their needs. Canned meats, fish, oysters, and clams were in some demand. An unemployed father of seven children, whom Stevey met on the ship *Independence*, did not seem concerned. "Everything I need for my family I can grow in my garden," he said.

Wairokai was bone-dry. No alcoholic beverages or native brews (that I was aware of) were used by the people, nor were they offered for sale. This probably was the result of the high cost of importing liquor and the strong influence of the church on village life. Some of the older men and women chewed betelnut, but the younger generations seemed to have completely rejected the habit. Pipe smoking, however, was popular with men and women.

Wairokai was a religious village, meaning that practically all of its inhabitants belonged to the South Seas Evangelical church. Nearby villages followed the same pattern, some being all Catholic, all Seventh Day Adventist, or some other church denomination. From what I observed, the church was the center of the social life of the people of Wairokai. Almost every morning at six o'clock a native drum sounded a call to worship. And every evening between 6:30 and 7:00 another service was held. On Sunday, this went on three times during the day. We attended a few services and were warmly received. Men sat on one side of the thatched building,

women on the other. In the meanwhile, small children crawled happily all over the dirt floor, chasing each other and stray dogs. While babies screamed and yelled, the congregation joyously stomped, clapped, and sang, oblivious to all disturbances.

There were always a few "heathens" in each village, people who cared nothing for the church and preferred their old customary way of life. These were usually older men who, at sometime in the past, may have been cannibals and headhunters and who practiced sorcery and witchcraft.

Every village seemed to have its own soccer field and Wairokai was no exception. The young men of the village played the game barefoot and with vigor and enthusiasm despite the intense heat. Among the girls, basketball was the favorite sport and almost every village had its own team.

We found that our major problem in acclimatizing ourselves to living in the Solomons was our susceptibility to skin infections. Unless immediately treated and bandaged, even the smallest cuts and bites became infected. Less adapted to the environment than the natives, our problems were accentuated. Wairokai had no medical help whatsoever, but at the nearby village of Rohinari, the Catholic church had established a mission hospital. No doctor was in residence, but a trained medical orderly gave penicillin shots and first aid. All too often, we found ourselves canoeing over to Rohinari for help.

Although we took our prescribed dosage of aralin once a week, malaria no longer seemed to be a major illness among the natives.

However, TB, worms, and skin ulcers are a scourge. Old "custom ways" once dictated that a woman must bear a child in a special bush house away from the village, where she had to spend some time both before and after delivery. Today, however, women from Wairokai go to the clinic of Rohinari where a specially trained nurse helps deliver babies under far more healthful conditions.

In Wairokai, as in all the other villages with which we became acquainted, the social and cultural life centered most exclusively around the church and family. The children appeared healthy and well cared for. There was no evidence of malnutrition.

While traveling the lagoon in our outboard-powered canoe, we often came across young boys fishing from their flimsy canoes, confidently handling themselves in the heavy seas around the numerous and every-present reefs. The fish they caught were always a welcome addition to the family table.

Every day of the week, except Sunday, the men and women would usually take off at about 7:30 A.M. to go to work in their gardens and return home at five. There were no rules. It was their garden and their responsibility. If they wanted to eat, they worked their gardens or starved. But people did come and go from their gardens as it pleased them. If there was no planting or harvesting to be done, their days were often spent in other activities or they rested.

We had a taste of what the garden work must be like when Samuel invited us to visit his own garden, which he explained, was only a *lic lic* (short) distance away. One hour later, after climbing a vertical jungle mountainside, we arrived at Samuel's garden. I marveled that elderly women used the trail almost daily, often carrying heavy loads of food and wood back to the village. To me, the trip was like climbing Mount Everest in mud. On arrival, we found Samuel's wife and children busily tending, cultivating, and harvesting his pepper plants and potatoes.

The reason was shortly explained for the planting of gardens in such poorly accessible locations. An absence of any appreciable amount of flat land along the coast has forced these people to clear land high upon the hills, often far from their villages, in order to grow enough food to sustain themselves.

As mentioned earlier, money was not a vital factor in this community, except for those who desired the more material things in life, and there were always those who did. Some liked to gamble, others wanted radios and wristwatches. A boat ticket to Honiara could be purchased with cash, which could be earned only by harvesting coconuts to produce copra, the only cash crop Wairokai had to offer.

Volumes could be written about the relationship between men and women in this society, but it is too complex a subject to discuss at length. Briefly, women definitely occupy a subordinate position to men. A woman might inherit property from her relatives, which would remain her own and she has her definite "rights" in the community life. However, the man is always the boss in family decision making.

Modern islanders recognize this disparity, but are in no hurry to change the rules, and there seems to be no evidence of a women's lib movement. While perhaps not content with their lot, most women accept this way of life.

The old "custom ways," practiced by the Solomon Islanders before the British took control, have largely been abandoned. Many of these customs were brutal, but on the whole "custom laws" fitted well the society for which they were designed.

The Malaitans were known in the early days as being extremely fierce and savage warriors. Other Solomon Islanders lived in fear of the Malaitans, who raided their villages for women, heads, and food, usually with great success. Cannibalism and headhunting were common until stamped out by the British years ago. There is evidence that sorcery and witchcraft are still practiced.

While visiting a small village near Wairokai, we were introduced to an elderly man, perhaps over eighty, although no one was certain of his age. He told us of his early life as a Namo before British law took hold. Japhlet translated for us, since the Namo spoke feebly in his native tongue. While he spoke, he was surrounded by an admiring group of men, women, and children.

The role of the Namos in early Malaitan culture was interesting. Here was a "custom" practice told to us in detail by one of its practitioners, a practice of such unique brutality as to deserve special attention.

To become a Namo, a man had to abandon all thoughts of living an ordinary life. He joined a cult of men whose sole purpose was to engage in professional killings. No ordinary man could fill this role, for the Namo had to be unusually quick, strong, and stealthy. In this role he must be constantly vigilant to escape retribution, with which he was constantly threatened.

Among the Malaitans, as in other societies, "payback" against a wrong to family or clan is a way of life. Revenge for that wrong must be satisfied. In the event of food or pig stealing, rape, adultery, injury or death, the wronged party engaged a Namo to kill the offender. Shell money was deposited with the Namo and increased until the Namo succeeded in doing his dirty work.

It was interesting and chilling to learn that it was not necessary for the Namo to kill the person having committed the offense. It was acceptable practice for the Namo to gain the revenge on almost anyone related to the offender—man, woman or child! Often women and children were ambushed and slaughtered. Their deaths were accepted as satisfying the required "payback." Our ancient friend bragged that he had killed five women and three men, much to the delight, if not the admiration, of the audience.

On most occasions, the Namos would then eat the flesh of those murdered. However, in the event of adultery, which was always punishable by death, the flesh was never eaten. The act was considered so vile that the adulterer's flesh was thought unclean.

As might be expected, the Namos themselves were subject to "payback." Consequently, these men usually banded together and lived a monastic life in isolated villages and islands where they could better protect themselves and their grisly profession.

During our week-long stay at Wairokai, I felt we could approach Japhlet and his brother Samuel (chief of the village) with the idea of returning at a later time for a lengthier visit. It was my hope that once I had reaffirmed the confidence of the village people and their leaders, they might give me permission to return and spend some time doing a more in-depth study and filming of their daily life.

I had already learned that the villagers did not readily accept strangers, especially those rushing around making films at every opportunity.

At one of the villages that Japhlet had taken us to visit, my request to take films was flatly refused. I appreciated their reasons and took no offense. I learned later that on some previous occasion a French writer-photographer had spent some time in the area. When he returned to France, he published an illustrated book about his experiences. Unfortunately, he made no effort to write and thank his hosts nor did he send them a copy of his book. The village chief had learned of this when he saw a copy of the book in a store while visiting Guadalcanal and felt incensed and slighted by this insensitivity.

Both Japhlet and Samuel seemed amenable to our return visit and the village council approved. Japhlet even proposed that when I was ready to return, he would take a leave of absence from his school teaching job so that we might journey around Malaita together, visiting and filming native life. Christmastime, he suggested, was the best for the visit because at that time all villages would be performing their traditional "custom" dances and ceremonies. Thus all the performances would be authentic—not just some rehearsal put on for a stranger.

It was even proposed at that time that for several hundred dollars the village would build us a house at Wairokai, which could be used for our headquarters for all future visits. I was quite thrilled with the idea and enjoyed contemplating telling my friends about my "little grass shack" on Malaita. Things really seemed to be shaping up.

On my return to California, I decided my best move would be to cement my relationship more firmly with Japhlet and the people of the village of Wairokai. My first act was to send Japhlet a check for three hundred dollars to be used "for the school."

I sent letters to all the important people I knew in the Solomon Islands: David Kusimae, member of parliament from Malaita; John Gina, a prominent politician and his brother Lloyd, speaker of the House; and David Ruthvin, Permanent Secretary of Cultural Affairs on Guadalcanal. It was my purpose to establish with these people the idea that I planned to return and would appreciate their assistance in receiving the necessary permits for my return trip to the Are Are Lagoon.

At first, all seemed to go well. Japhlet wrote to say that he had received the three hundred dollars and used it to buy a lawnmower for the school. This puzzled me somewhat. I had envisioned that the money might be better spent for books, blackboards, and other educational items. Stevey even responded to Japhlet's request and sent out several parcels of school books. My dreams of a South Sea island "hideaway paradise" seemed to be materializing.

Looking back, more in amusement than in anger, I watched everything go awry; Japhlet no longer answered my inquiries as the months went by. A political upheaval in the Solomons saw all of my old "contacts" either out of office or fired. No one answered my letters. Christmas was approaching, but without any firm assurance from anyone that I would be welcomed back to Wairokai, I disappointedly abandoned my plans.

Then came a puzzling letter from Japhlet asking me not to come to Wairokai. The letter seemed to say more between the lines. Stevey and I spent several hours trying to figure out what Japhlet was trying to tell us in his poor, hastily written letter. Finally, a dim picture emerged that went something like this: "Japhlet had received the three hundred dollars and had proudly announced to the village the fact. He may or may not have promised to buy a lawnmower for the school, but temptation got the best of him and he pocketed the money for his own use. As Japhlet rather sadly explained in his letter, 'The cheque you sent me, I have received it. However, the money was used by me and a few people from my village are complaining about it. I'm still trying to settle the matter and might

be taken to court. I have quit my job at the school in
Wairokai. Someone from Wairokai will be writing you
making inquiries about the personal cheque you sent
me—just keep quiet and have nothing to say. I shall try
to resign my job to work with you.' " That letter was
written some time ago. Since then, I haven't heard anything from Japhlet.

## *Chapter Fourteen*

# Rebellion on Vanuatu

It was now 1980. Once again I was determined to return to Tanna to see once again the John Frum festival and try and penetrate more of the mysteries of this strange cult and see what time might have wrought.

I suffered the usual snafus starting the trip. I arrived at the Los Angeles airport carrying my wife's passport and missed the flight. At this point I sensed that Murphy's Law might be going into effect. How right I was.

I caught up with my traveling companion, Bill Lyte, at Port Vila where we made a brief stay at the old, reliable Hotel Rossi while awaiting transportation to Tanna.

A cruise ship was in the harbor and the town was crowded with tourists. Bill and I retreated to the veranda of the Rossi for an evening beer. A cool breeze was blowing in from the ocean and the cumulus clouds were piled up like mountains out over the bay. We enjoyed watching them as they turned from flaming red to soft pink and finally an indigo blue.

The weather cleared long enough for flight service to resume to Tanna, and once again I headed south to this mystical island. The flight was without incident, but from there on there was nothing but trouble.

Bill Lyte and I were staying at Russell Paul's place near the village of Lanakel, waiting for transportation to

Sulphur Bay where the festival is always held. Lounging in Russell's home over a warm beer, I overheard the sounds of hammering and pounding nearby. I asked Russell, "Are you building new quarters?"

"No," he answered, "the natives are tearing down my workshed to make clubs and shields."

The next few days on Tanna we saw signs of furious activity between rival political factions on the island. There were rumors of dynamite charges being placed at roadblocks. I witnessed a confrontation at the grass airstrip upon the arrival of the French commissioner, Jean-Jacques Rober. Three armed groups of men showed up—forty men on horseback armed with spears, another twenty men standing in a tight formation armed with clubs and bows and arrows, and a third group giving us dirty looks and loud shouts.

Bill and I carefully hurried around with our camera and tape recorders, avoiding too close a contact with the irate natives who were now engaged in a loud shouting match as they surrounded the newly arrived French commissioner. Our traveling friend, Max, approached an angry orator and was told to "to bugger off" in pidgin, which sounds exactly the same in English. Max got the message and hastily departed.

The unusual "condominium" government of the New Hebrides, now Vanuatu, was, until independence in July 1980, ruled jointly by both Great Britain and France. In 1979, these joint powers agreed to grant the seventy-island chain of islands independence.

Pre-independence elections were held and a parliament was selected, headed by Prime Minister-elect Walter Lini, a Melanesian as well as an Anglican priest.

Lini's nationalist, predominantly English-speaking Vanuaaku party won the election, but the victory was resented by planters on French-dominated Espiritu Santo. Their anger increased when Lini promised to carry out land reforms that would break up the island's large plantations.

The new government-elect headquarters were located at Port Vila on the island of Efate, some two hundred miles south of Espiritu Santo. Port Vila is remembered by many American veterans as one of the important staging areas for Allied troups preparing for the invasion of Guadalcanal. Today Efate is probably the richest and most influential island of Vanuatu.

European colonists created artificial island nations in the South Seas over the centuries. New Guinea, the largest island in the South Pacific, with a population over two million people, knows of seven hundred separate and distinct languages! On the tiny island of Tanna, where we were staying, there are ten different languages! So there is little point in thinking that a great deal of homogeneity exists among the people of these island nations.

As the time for independence approached, resentment toward the government-elect continued to grow and finally erupted into open revolt on Espiritu Santo. The principal leader of the revolt was Jimmy Stevens, a bearded man of Scottish and native ancestry, who claimed that he and his followers only wanted to rule themselves. "Vila is Vila, Santo is Santo—different language, different customs," Stevens said.

A new and interesting report, however, clouded his separatist claims. A Carson City, Nevada, land developer by the name of Michael Oliver claimed in June of 1980 that the separatist rebellion on the island of Espiritu Santo was planned and financed by his real estate subdivision office a couple of blocks from the Nevada state capitol.

Oliver had a reputation as a promoter attempting to find small, tax-free independent nations in the Caribbean and the South Seas. Oliver also claimed (as reported in the *Los Angeles Times* in June of 1980) that he had know Jimmy Stevens for over ten years and that Stevens had frequently flown to Carson City to discuss with him the formation of an independent government on Espiritu Santo, with Stevens as prime minister.

Basically, Oliver justified his interference by stating that he only wanted to help prevent Vanuatu from falling into the communist orbit. In fact, it is reported that Lini had made several trips to Soviet bloc nations as the guest of communist countries. If Jimmy Stevens's revolt succeeded, he planned to set up a government based on the principles of the Libertarian Party known in the United States. Oliver admits to having given the rebel leaders on Santo $120,000 to finance the rebellion. Since the rebellion, nothing more has been heard from Oliver.

While the revolt eventually failed, it provided several months of distress throughout the islands. Jimmy Stevens assembled a force of about five hundred natives and fifty French-speaking islanders and declared himself the prime minister of the nation of Vemerama. The first act of violence occurred when a local British police officer tried to fire a tear gas grenade at the rebels. He received an arrow in his butt for his troubles, the first reported casualty of the rebellion.

Jimmy continued to insist that he only wanted to restore the land to its traditional tribal owners and prevent Lini's government from nationalizing the land. However, his association with Oliver led to suspicions that he may have wanted to turn the island into a tax-free haven with gambling casinos, land development projects and other enterprises.

It was into this festering revolt that we walked without the slightest knowledge that there was any trouble on Tanna except the usual plagues of flies, mosquitoes, and heavy rains. Fortunately for us, we were living on one of Russell's isolated huts near the beach and away from the battle zone. Russell was afraid to let his jeep out on the road, effectively depriving us of any transport for most of the time. The nearest village to us was Lanakel, four or five miles away, and our only source of food. We were often forced to hitch rides on trucks that occasionally passed by.

The climax on Tanna came when about two hundred John Frumers stormed the government offices. Local police used tear gas against the rioters. One man was killed and numerous others received spear and arrow wounds and bloody heads before twenty-five British and French police were airlifted to Tanna to put down the uprising. This all occurred after we had left the island, but it was plain to see what was coming. The feelings on Tanna were much the same as those expressed by Jimmy Stevens. "Different language, different customs." The Tannese had no use for the crowd running the show in Vila and wanted to set up their own independence.

Meanwhile, in the north, Prime Minister-elect Walter Lini was finally getting some help. Two hundred British and French paratroopers landed in Espiritu Santo and occupied Luganville, the main town, without firing a shot. Jimmy Stevens, defiant as ever, retreated to his jungle hideout at Vanafoa, north of Espiritu Santo.

At this point, Lini invited troops from neighboring Papua New Guinea to replace the British and French paratroopers, which they did, landing about four hundred soldiers on Espiritu Santo and taking up positions around Stevens' headquarters. There is no doubt that Lini felt more comfortable with the British and French troops out. The islands had been subject to seventy-eight years of colonial rule and it was time to see their military presence gone before they might decide to change their minds and retake this trouble-plagued nation.

The handwriting was on the wall and Jimmy Stevens must have seen it. His worst blow came when troops killed his son as he tried to break a roadblock set up around rebel headquarters. This occurred in August of 1980. To the best of my knowledge, this fatality and the one on Tanna were the only deaths during the revolution.

Jimmy Stevens, facing overwhelming odds, finally surrendered. After all, most of his rebels were armed with little more than sticks, stones, spears, and bows and arrows, hardly a match for well-trained army troops. Vanuatu proclaimed its independence on July 30, 1980, just shortly before the rebellion was completely suppressed. But troubles and problems remained.

All along, the new government of Vanuatu suspected the French government of some complicity with Jimmy Stevens and his rebels. After all, Espiritu Santo had a large French community, French was the local language, and the French wanted to retain strong economic ties in the area.

Vanuatu-French relations deteriorated fast in the first days of February 1981, with Vanuatu declaring French ambassador Yves Rodrigues *persona non grata* and giving him twenty-four hours to leave the country. In retaliation, a senior French spokesman threatened to cancel completely the promised French financial aid to the infant republic. A sizable number of French settlers were asked to leave the country and did so.

Not too much had changed since I had last seen Sulphur Bay. The weather, to be expected, was abominable. It was raining cats and dogs. Since my camera was broken, I retired to the nearest hut for a repair job while Bill and Max busied themselves taking pictures of the festival activities.

It seemed even more evident now that most of the admonitions of John Frum were either ignored or forgotten by the celebrants. The women wore colorful dresses and the men were garbed in T-shirts and shorts. European goods and hard liquor could be bought at the trade store for hard cash. Many of the festival dances, accompanied by guitar, had a Polynesian flavor. People proudly wore their yellow T-shirts marked with the "John Frum, United Conservative New Hebrides Party." Nearby, a small Christian church displayed the symbolic red cross of John Frum and a picture of Jesus Christ. Above the display was a large picture of all the American astronauts superimposed on the surface of the moon. The faithful church members, mixing a little bit of Christianity with some John Frumism, claimed that they had predicted that the Americans would be the first people to land on the moon!

A few of the older people still do believe that John Frum lives and that he is in America collecting the cargo to bring back to the people of Tanna. Some are skeptical. Many, however, have accepted the Christian faith. For them, John Frum can no longer be accepted as the returning messiah. But his legend remains strong and provides a binding force for the people.

Today, the people of Tanna are prosperous and reasonably contented. The white man has gone and they have achieved their independence as a nation. Cargo comes every day by ships and planes. Almost everyone owns a transistor radio, a bicycle, or a pair of shoes. The myth of John Frum still remains, however. Was there really ever a John Frum? Some say they heard him speak. Some say he was black, others say that he was white. Regardless of whether he was a messiah, a myth, or just a man, he provided at one time in history a faith to a people that needed to believe in themselves.

## *Chapter Fifteen*

# The Land Divers of Pentecost Island

Athough traveling and filming in such faraway places as the ice cap of Greenland and the cave paintings of the Sahara Desert, the strange cults of the South Seas were forever on my mind.

Another curious cult on the island of Pentecost, Vanuatu, began to attract my attention. In death defying actions, men would leap from eighty-foot high towers, barely saving their lives as vines attached to their ankles arrested their fall. This I was determined to see.

There are many legends behind the Land Divers of the village of Bunlap on the island of Pentecost in the South Seas but they all follow a general theme. One legend goes that a woman in the village was being mistreated by her husband. In desperation, she fled the village to hide in the jungle. Knowing that her husband would follow her, she climbed the highest tree she could find. Planning carefully she tied lengthy liana vines to her ankles. The husband finally arrived, shouting abuses and threats. He climbed the tree after his wife and grabbed wildly for her. She jumped and he fell after her. The vines arrested her fall before she hit the earth. The husband, however, hit the earth, breaking his neck. The men of Bunlap were furious at this shame inflicted on them by a woman and decided to make the land diving an all-male event as a test of manhood and courage.

In 1981, I was corresponding with Kirk Huffman, the head curator of the Museum in Port Vila, Vanuatu, in hopes that he might assist me in making arrangements to witness this unusual ceremony. The jumps occur only once a year at the village of Bunlap on the southwest coast of Pentecost Island. The timing of the event is critical because the liana vines must have reached their maximum solidity as well as elasticity. This occurs sometime during the middle of May, shortly after the yams in the village gardens have been harvested. Local tradition says that successful jumps are indispensable for satisfactory yam gardens for the following year.

Twice I was on the telephone to Port Vila discussing with Kirk when the tower jumping at Bunlap might occur, but finally, in late April, he said, "The jumps will occur May 15, but allow yourself some leeway, for Pentecost is not an easy place to reach, especially if the weather is bad."

Stevey and I left Los Angeles May 9, 1982, and with only a brief overnight stopover in Fiji found ourselves once again on our old stomping grounds at Port Vila. We had planned our stay at the old and reliable Hotel Rossi, but new construction work there made the noise so intolerable that we moved on to quieter quarters. Even then, we often returned to the Rossi for a late afternoon beer on the terrace where one could enjoy the enchanting sunsets.

Things had changed in Vanuatu since my last visit in February of 1980. The country had achieved its independence from Great Britain and France; it had survived Jimmy Stevens's revolution on Espiritu Santo; and tourism was showing a booming increase, especially on the island of Efate.

I was surprised to find the weather pleasantly cool

most of the time, not the usual enervating heat that sapped both mind and body. A weak cyclone was passing through the area and the weather remained overcast and rainy.

By a stroke of luck I caught Kirk at the museum. The next day he and his wife would be off on a two-month trip to South America and Europe. I was disappointed because I was counting on Kirk's knowledge and expertise as an anthropologist to explain many of the quaint customs and traditions relating to the people of Bunlap and their land-diving ceremony. Fortunately, however, he had time for a beer at the Hotel Rossi with us. After several beers and two hours of conversation, we all felt Kirk's enthusiasm for his research work. He turned us over to his assistant, Jack Kadate, whom he was training to take over his position.

The next day while passing government offices, I noticed the new flag of Vanuatu flying proudly from the flagpole. A yellow colored Y runs the horizontal length of the flag with three fields of red, green, and black filling the space between. In the corner is a circular pig's tusk. In Vanuatu society, the circular pig's tusk represents the most important item that anyone can own.

The curved boar's tooth is the result of a long and patient process that takes years to develop. The upper canine teeth of the pig is split when the animal is young; its lower tusks then tend to grow in the desired circular form. The more circles formed, the more valuable the tusk. Suffice it to say that the pig must suffer horribly from this treatment and most are unable to feed themselves and must be hand fed—this is always the women's duty.*

* In most South Pacific Islands, the bride price for a woman includes a large number of pigs, as well as tusks, shells, and sometimes cash.

Vanuatu culture, in the old, traditional custom system, has been explained as one of *pig, power,* and *prestige.**
A man buys his wife or wives with pigs; the wives raise the pigs; the pigs can buy more wives, and with more wives and more pigs than anyone else a man can gain great power and prestige in his community.

At the village of Bunlap, the social organization of the village is founded upon a hierarchy of grades. Chieftainship has no hereditary rights. During the course of their lifetime in the village, men pass through different "grades." Those who attain the highest rung on the social ladder have the greatest power and prestige in the community.

In order to pass from one grade to another, a man must be able to make gifts of a certain number of pigs. The number and value of the pigs are proportional to the importance of the grade. The Big Man, as these important chiefs are sometimes called, shares in the decisions that determine the community's social and cultural life, decides the punishment for a crime, and declares when to make war.

We completed our arrangements for the trip to Pentecost on May 14. Both Stevey and I were apprehensive about the weather conditions. The trip would involve traveling by plane, truck, boat, and on foot. The seas were turning rough and the wind was rising. If a plane or boat couldn't make it, we were stuck, for Pentecost is an isolated island with only a rundown grass airstrip.

We arose at 4:30 on the morning of May 15 with instructions to be at the airport for our chartered flight at 6:30. We arrived in good time to find the airport locked up tight. Only a sliver of light was showing on the horizon.

*Karl Muller's book and information.

At about 6:00 A.M., the rest of the passengers on our charter began to arrive. Eight of us remained around the still locked airport, discussing the prospects of taking off.

Help finally came in the form of the airport concessionnaire who revived us with stale coffee, weak tea, and an assortment of dried biscuits. Some arriving passengers for other flights were fortifying their courage with a morning beer or two.

Our ten-passenger, twin-engined Otter had been taxied out on the tarmac awaiting the arrival of our pilot, who was nowhere to be seen. By 7:30 we were worried because we still had a long journey ahead of us, even after landing at Pentecost's Lonorora airstrip.

By 8:00 A.M. we were getting desperate. The pilot was not answering his telephone. Some knowing airport clerk suggested that he might have spent the night at his girl friend's house. A taxi was finally dispatched to locate him. He arrived shortly at the airport, to our rousing applause. He apologetically explained that no one had told him that he was to fly a charter flight that day. He laconically commented to our group, as we streamed nervously on board the plane, "This matter shall be thoroughly investigated and innocent heads will fall."

The one-hour flight to Lonorora was uneventful but the skies were cloudy and the sea looked rough, especially around southern Pentecost where we would be seaborn in a few hours.

A pick-up truck met us at Lonorora, loading us into the back with our assortment of cameras, duffle bags, and knapsacks. It was a rough, uncomfortable forty-five-minute drive down the west coast of Pentecost to the village of Pangi where our boat would meet us. The countryside was beautifully green with many cattle grazing and bountiful gardens of taro and breadfruit. On the way we passed over a sulfur spring trickling into the sea and at the few villages we saw, hoards of kids rushed out to greet us.

Our boat, which greeted my eyes on arriving at Pangi, at first seemed too small to be believed. I thought that it was there to transfer us out to some larger vessel lying offshore. That was not to be the case, however, and we crowded into this eighteen-foot-long battered old tub and were consigned to the mercy of the sea.

At first, most of the passengers crowded into the cabin top, for the fumes from the ancient diesel engine were sickening. A few of us stayed in the open-sided cabin below. I could barely tolerate the fumes myself, but I knew I wanted a good seat when the weather roughened, which I was sure it would.

The floor of the cabin had been thoughtfully covered with several layers of palm fronds to protect our feet from the bilge water, or so I thought. As I sat there, Stevey exclaimed, "Your foot's bleeding." I lifted up my blood-soaked tennis shoe in puzzlement, for I felt no pain. Closer examination showed that the palm fronds were not there to protect our feet but, rather, to cover the head and various parts of a full-size, newly butchered cow. Had I known that it was also to be our dinner that night, I might have given the matter more thought.

The trip around southern Pentecost to Bunlap took us three and a half hours. Rounding the tip of the island, the seas were rough, but the native skipper seemed competent and sure of himself. There were no life jackets on board. Not that it probably mattered for most of the coast line consisted of jagged, menacing rocks and I couldn't see much chance of our surviving a shipwreck.

Rounding the cape, another half hour brought us into Barrier Bay. The small village of Bunlap appeared in the distance. However, it was not our destination since we were to land on the beach near the trail that led to the jump tower. Willing native hands helped us through the surf, along with our gear and, of course, our beef dinner.

Because of the delay of our flight and our longer-than-anticipated boat trip, when we arrived the villagers on the beach told us that the jumps were already under way and we would have to hurry to see what was left of the ceremony. What followed was a foot race up a steep, slippery mountain trail, most of us stumbling, sliding, and falling all the way.

Halfway up, Stevey called back and said, "We've forgotten the tape recorder." I said, "Forget it, that's too far back." Later, after we had reached the top, our guide sent a young boy back to retrieve it from the beach. It took him two trips to get the right equipment, but the effort was well worth it because of the sound effects of the dancing and singing that we were able to tape were magnificent.

*Chapter Sixteen*

# The Jump

The first sight to greet us as we arrived at the top was the tower, standing some eighty feet into the air. On a flat hill back of the tower, men danced and chanted while women whistled through their teeth, swaying their bodies back and forth. A fairly large crowd of several hundred people had gathered to watch, including a small number of Europeans. The native men were clothed with only a penis sheath that was carefully tucked into a fiber belt worn around the waist. The women wore the traditional grass skirts and shell beads around their necks.

The tower and the liana vines are the important support system for the jumpers. The lianas must have reached their maximum solidity and elasticity. This depends upon the amount of rain and sunshine received while growing. If the lianas are not right, jumpers can be injured and this would not augur well for next year's yam crop.

Once the liana is hung from the tower, it is called the *tal*. The ends attached to the jumper's ankles are split into many strands and wrapped in banana leaves to help them remain pliable and moist before the jump.

The construction of the tower takes place some sixty days before the land-diving ceremony so it was not possible for me to witness this. By good fortune Stevey discovered Karl Muller's notes on this in the library at Port Vila, and I am indebted to Karl for this information.*

*Karl Muller is a noted authority on the ceremony.

"The first man to cut down the tree to be used as the main, vertical support for the tower becomes the 'boss' of the tower construction. He determines the general plan of construction with other, older, more experienced men. He also earns the privilege of jumping from the highest platform although he often relinquishes this privilege.

"There are usually twelve central vertical supports to the tower buried three or four feet underground and extending thirty-eight feet above the ground. Over two miles of liana vines are used to tie the supporting parts of the tower together. The final result looks like a jumble of twisted and interlocking bits of wood and vine stretching eighty feet into the air. A series of lengthy guy ropes made of native vines are attched to the rear of the tower and planted in the hill behind. This is to prevent the structure from being toppled in a strong wind.

"Narrow platforms jut out at ascending intervals, usually about six feet apart. These are the jumping platforms and are constructed by the men who jump from them. The young boys and less experienced jumpers dive from the lower platforms while the older and more experienced divers will jump from sixty to eighty feet, depending on their courage.

"The names of the parts of the tower correspond to the parts of the human body. The whole tower is called in the native language *tarebe* (body). The sides are called *sigol*, the cross braces *sinte*, the ribs *ban*, the back *alugal*, and the interior *lontegal*. The platforms are named after sexual organs of the male body.

"While the tower is under construction, the men sing and chant to keep up the work tempo. It is absolutely taboo for women to come close to the construction site. During this period, all sexual relationships between men and women must cease.

"After the tower has been completed an *armat* or

spirit will come to inhabit it. The people know this by the crackling noises they hear in the tower and the tingling sensation in their skins and pulsations in their bodies.

"The ground at the foot of the tower is not flat but slopes down at about a twenty-degree angle. It is thoroughly dug up and churned to a depth of about one foot. Throughout the day of the jump, I watched two men continually churning the ground at the foot of the tower.

"The night before the land-diving ceremony takes place the men of the village stay by the tower to prevent 'poison men' from pushing evil spirits into the softened ground. The day of the ceremony the men go down to the sea for a ritual bath—afterwards rubbing coconut oil all over their bodies. The costume for the jumpers is simple. The only clothing is a *nambus* (penis sheath) wrapped around the penis and tucked into a fiber belt around the waist. Most of the men wore a set of pig's tusks hung around the neck while some of the higher grade men wore cyca leaves in their belts and streaked their faces with a reddish clay called *pripri*."

In the morning the young boys jumped. We missed this because of our late arrival. I was told that a young boy the age of five dove from a twenty-three-foot platform. However, it should be remembered that although this is a once-a-year ceremony, practicing for the event never ceases.

Upon arriving at the jump site, out of breath and covered with mud, I struggled around the steep, muddy slope looking for a secure footing from which to film while Stevey raced off with the tape recorder to get the sound effects from the dancers.

The singing and dancing was impressive. On a flat hill at the back of the tower and about fifteen feet away, a large group of fifty or sixty men and women were chanting, dancing, stomping, and whistling. The men and women danced in separate groups, the men closer to the tower.

There were two variants to the dancing. The men and women either stood in place, stomping one foot, or danced back and forth, three steps to either side. The women whistled through their teeth while the men sang a series of songs punctuated by yells and shouts. As the jumper stood on his platform readying for his leap, the whistling, singing, and stomping increased in intensity to give the jumper greater courage. When he jumped all sound ceased.

The first jump I witnessed was from about seventy feet. The jumper carefully made his way up the tower to his platform where his toes hugged the edge while his assistants knotted the vines to his ankles and made certain that the vines would not tangle with the tower during his descent. As primitive as the whole operation seemed, each land diver's lianas had been so carefully measured that the vines would become taunt and jerk him upwards just as his head touched the ground! I watched spellbound as the jumper untucked a leave from his belt and holding it away from his body, let it fall. It was said that if a girl caught the leaf, she could sleep with the jumper but would not be obliged to marry him.

A crescendo of sound was beating the air encouraging the jumper to make his leap. I strained my neck backwards once again to watch the jumper. Now he was clasping his hands, praying to his sun god.* The atmosphere was tense as all eyes strained to watch the jumper. My

* The people of Bunlap are pagans and the jumpers call upon their sun gods to give them courage and success.

heart was in my mouth as he arched his back for the final time and then slowly toppled forward in space. His descent was uninterrupted, appearing to be in slow motion, until the last fraction of a second when the vines around his ankles catapulted him back into the air about six feet, his jumping platform snapping off as the vines stretched to their utmost. His head had barely brushed the ground!

Men standing at the foot of the tower rushed out to grab the diver as he was jerked up to prevent him from crashing back into the tower. The diver's lianas were cut off his ankles and he was carried off to the side to be congratulated by his friends and relatives. The wife of the jumper, however, was never allowed to join in the congratulations lest she be thought too eager for her husband.

For the rest of the afternoon the land diving continued. Some jumps were performed gracefully, others clumsily—as might be expected in any sporting event. I was told that if a man lost courage and could not complete his jump, it was no disgrace, but on this day no one backed off.

Many strange customs were observed. After a young man completed his jump his mother rushed over to him and danced around with an imitation baby in her arms, which she promptly threw away. This symbolized that her son had now become a man.

One jumper had a vine break on one ankle and he landed on his back. His fall had been mostly arrested and he managed to walk away although it was obvious that he was in pain. When his women relatives witnessed this they went into loud wailing but when it was discovered that he was not dangerously injured, the wailing stopped, as if by orchestration.

One young man must have bumped his head on the

edge of the tower. He sat down on the slope with a dazed, uncomprehending look on his face. After his mother had comforted him, an older man came over and engaged him in quiet conversation. The speechless young man kept nodding his head. I didn't understand the language but had no doubts that the older man was giving him some coaching advice. I couldn't help compare the scene with an American coach giving his gymnast quiet advice after a bad tumble.

Twenty-three jumps were performed at Bunlap that day with only one injury that I observed. How many men suffered from pulled thigh and ankle muscles, it is hard to say, but there must have been some.

A lull set in while the final jumper made his way up the tower and carefully prepared his platform and lianas. This was the climax, a spectacular leap from the highest platform at eighty-one feet to be performed by Bunlap's best land diver.

Slowly the sound from the crowd began to build up to a crescendo as the jumper watched his helpers clear the liana vines from any possible entanglement with the tower. Suddenly the crowd and the singers became very quiet while the jumper, standing on his platform, began to address the assembled people.

Native custom dictates that the final (and best) land diver may say anything he wishes to. He is free to speak his mind. If he wishes, he can complain about his wife's behavior, unjust treatment by fellow villagers, and a host of other comments. His was a lengthy speech, none of which I understood, but it seemed to be appreciated by the crowd.

The final jump was perfectly executed and what followed reminded me of the actions of a victorious football team when one of their men has just caught the winning touchdown pass in the final seconds of the Rose Bowl game. Fellow villagers rushed out and swarmed around the jumper and hoisted him into the air, shouting and jumping in a victory dance. It was an exciting moment, the climax of a long day, and an assurance of a good yam crop for the next year.

Within minutes the land-diving area had been cleared, with the villagers all returning to Bunlap to feast and drink kava. We made our way down the mountain and spent the night at the native guest house on the beach. We were not welcome in Bunlap. The dinner of meat and rice was close to inedible despite our hunger. Sleep was impossible. A group of Bunlapers had decided to continue their celebration near the guest house and the uproar continued from dusk till dawn. They were very drunk on kava and beer and were having an uproariously good time.

Our boat returned us to Pangi under menacing skies and in dangerous seas. We bailed the whole way. The weather was definitely worsening and some visitors found their boat skippers unwilling to risk the high seas. They spent the night in a wild trek across the mountains from Bunlap to the airstrip in Lonorora. The edge of the cyclone was sweeping past Vanuatu and we realized that if the land-diving event had been held one day later, we would never have reached Pentecost Island to witness this spectacular ceremony. The sun god must also have shone on us.

The native people of the South Seas have a heritage and a culture that is rich and imaginative. While some of their old customs seem bizarre and unexplainable to us, they were the results of the people adapting their lives to circumstances surrounding their times.

To quote Carl Sagan, "We all learn to adapt and

change. It would be sad to think that our past could not be an important part of our future."

In all of my travels I have learned one important thing. There is no superior race, only superior people. Each of us lives within our own culture. To destroy culture is to destroy mankind.